THE LIBRARY BOOK

P

PROFILE BOOKS

The Library Book is published in support of
The Reading Agency

First published in 2012 by
Profile Books Ltd,
3A Exmouth House,
Pine Street,
London ECIR 0JH

A complete catalogue record for this book can be
obtained from the British Library on request

ISBN 978 1 78125 005 1
eISBN 978 1 84765 840 1

Designed and typeset by Crow Books
Printed and bound in Great Britain by Clays, Bungay, Suffolk

CONTENTS

CONTENTS

FOREWORD

REBECCA GRAY

The Library Book began with a simple idea: to celebrate libraries. As the book took shape, it became clear that the value of public libraries transcends the books on the shelves. Books and stories are lifelines, and libraries house those lifelines, making them available to all. They are important not just for the books, but for the space and freedom they provide, as well as the navigation and advice provided by librarians.

I volunteer for a project run by Quaker Homeless Action, a mobile library. One of my colleagues, John, is, in his own words, a poacher-turned-gamekeeper. John used to borrow books from the library every week. The volunteers always looked forward to seeing him – he's an enthusiastic reader, and we'd always have a good chat about the books he'd read, and what he might read next. Now he has a home, and he volunteers almost as often as he used to borrow books. Many of the people who visit us at the mobile library know John, and he's become a bit of a draw. People come to the library to say hello, have a catch up, and often, they'll end up borrowing a book too.

It's perhaps surprising that about half the books we lend are returned, not a bad statistic given that most of our borrowers are itinerant. John says it's a symbol of trust that when you're on the streets, and someone lends you a book, it builds your confidence and becomes an emotional investment. We've had books returned, carefully wrapped in protective plastic, so that they've stayed dry when the person who read them is soaking wet from the winter weather. Sometimes, though they have nothing of their own, our readers donate the books they've been given elsewhere to be added to our library.

For many of us, borrowers and volunteers alike, the mobile library is a meeting point, a place where all sorts of people come together, to have conversations you'd never imagined, hear life stories that seem completely different to yours, or surprisingly familiar. Like all libraries, it's a place where our minds open up, and the world becomes a little wider, and yet smaller too. John's description of it is perfect: 'You go to the library on your own, but you end up talking to people, the librarians, other readers. And a conversation about a book becomes one about life, and you leave feeling that you aren't alone after all.'

At the library, some of the people who share our city but are mostly ignored become fellow book-lovers, and it's a great equaliser. In the rest of their lives, they are asking for help, or being told what to do; here they are just people who are welcome to take a book. And when you take away a book, you're taking an escape route from your own problems, or from the boredom of empty hours. John describes the library as a combination of things: it's a place where practical things – information, face-to-face contact, filling your time – combine with elements that are harder to pin down, like escapism, imagination and comfort.

John found that, as a homeless man, he was often perceived as a threat, or a nuisance. He says that the library made him feel part of a network, he made friends, and that gave him confidence, and the ability to trust people, where he'd had none before. And those things helped him get back on track, so that now he has a place of his own, and a library card too. More than anything else though, the library has taught me and John that – with apologies for the cliché – you can never judge a book by its cover. What people want to read often seems incongruous. A pair of biker-types taking away *Thoughts of the Dalai Lama*. People without access to instruments requesting sheet music. Aspiring poets sharing their work and then borrowing horror stories.

Putting this book together – as well as working

on the mobile library with John – has been truly enlightening. So many people who write books would never have even begun reading without the influence of these completely democratic public spaces. So many of the writers who've contributed describe the library as a place of liberation, a place where lives literally change, and change in a way infinitely more profound – and common – than in any other place I can think of. So I'm very grateful indeed that so many authors have kindly given their work to this book, and their royalties to The Reading Agency. That money will go to their library programmes, which are described at the end of this book. By buying, or borrowing, this book, you're already supporting The Reading Agency, but if you'd like to know more about their work, do visit www.thereadingagency.org.uk

I hope you enjoy *The Library Book*.

THIS PLACE WILL LEND YOU BOOKS FOR FREE

JAMES BROWN

Do you read books? Hundreds of them? Are your shelves, rooms, bags, cars, offices full of books? Do you buy them on impulse at train stations and airports? Read the first few chapters before your journey ends? Do you come across a car-boot sale, second-hand bookshop or a charity shop; and walk away with books that look like bargains but only have a 25 per cent chance of getting read?

Do you hunger for new releases by favourite writers, get lost scouring Amazon and eBay and fan sites for rare editions, or volumes you only just heard about? Then never buy them. Go through books in a night, a week, one sitting. Lose sleep over them. Clinging on till the very end. An end that leaves you in tears, angry or spent? Or do they drag on for months and months while other easier-to-digest stories come and go?

Do you look forward to holidays because you know there'll be a literary lottery on the hotel's second-hand library shelf? Do you buy books like a habit? Do you find it hard to move them on after you've read them, caught between wanting to give them to a friend, or get some of the cover value back, and wanting to retain them as a physical memory of the time you enjoyed reading them?

I do a lot of that and more. You can also add the following to books I have: presents I receive, the books I borrow from friends, and the ones that arrive from publishers and writers. But I did something on Saturday that might change all that. I joined a library. And I was shocked, exhilarated and inspired by the experience.

The library in question has been there for a short while, in the high street of a small town I visit regularly, Rye in East Sussex. It is less than a year old, a huge, clean, well-stocked affair that now sits in what used to be Woolworths. It has computers, computer games, DVDs, talking books and most importantly, books. Thousands of them and, as my son, my girlfriend and I all individually noticed, hardly any of the books have ever been taken out. It couldn't be more different from the libraries I remember from years gone by.

When I suggested joining the library my girlfriend laughed at me, and accused me of looking for a money-saving scheme, but it just seemed to make sense. I'd walked past this big double-fronted shop full of literature many times and hadn't bothered to venture in. Meanwhile I was suggesting going to a table sale just to see if an old lady I'd once talked to had any more Rebus crime novels and the g/f was getting antsy because she'd run out of books by an author she was consuming at a rate of one every forty-eight hours.

I've not been a member of a library since I was about ten years old so I wasn't too sure what to expect, but I figured you'd have to pay something to join and something to take each book out and it would take ages like everything else does to join or sign up for nowadays. So I was stunned when the lady behind the counter explained it was free to take a book out, free to join and you could prolong your borrowing of a particular book beyond the three-week deadline online. Plus you can order a book and they'll get it in for you for 8op. So that was it, all of it's free. No wonder those that use libraries regularly are up in arms about proposed closures of them. It just strikes me as something a nation can boast about – we lend people books for free.

A couple of forms filled in, a card signed, a proof of address and boom we were in. Crime books – masses of them – le Carré, Michael Connelly, Elmore Leonard, James Ellroy, David Peace. History books, war books, books by Sabotage Times writers, sports books. I'm not too sure what my girlfriend was examining at the time, but my son was just staring at all the books and films, wondering what to take. It was like being in Waterstones, but free. Eventually I had to call time on the browsing as we were running out of reading hours. We left with a Michael Connolly thriller, an early le Carré novel, a kids' book and the *Diary of A Wimpy Kid* film.

Back home to read, great books in hand, no money spent and knowing the house won't have yet more books in that no one else ever gets to read. Next time you're driving or walking past your local library maybe break the habit and step inside. It's even cheaper than Amazon.

CHARACTER BUILDING

ANITA ANAND

I still can't open a book without smelling chlorine and tomato soup. It was a ritual for us throughout our childhood. Three noisy siblings being taken by a weary mother for a weekend of character building. First there was swimming at the Loughton swimming pools, where bombing and heavy petting were strictly prohibited, but running around the pool was largely ignored by the indifferent Essex lifeguards. Then instant soup from the machines in the foyer. The fewer powdery lumps at the bottom of the plastic cup, the luckier the week ahead was going to be.

And then, best bit of all. The part that made the stinging eyes, lumpy soup and clammy, clinging tights all worthwhile. The library was the best place in the world. A labyrinth of shelves where you could lose your mother and then lose yourself in a book of Greek myths, or somebody's struggle to find love in class 5C or the life-cycle of a ladybird. At the age of around seven, I had decided that I would read every single book in Loughton Library. And at first the mission was a febrile one. My poor mum would find me behind two piles of books, refusing to go home unless I could finish reading the one pile and take the other home. I'm certain my present and permanent shoulder ache is a result of winning those weekly battles and the hefting that came with such victory.

During that time, an awkward schoolgirl (who found herself out of the class more than in it – normally excluded for chatting and generally irritating behaviour), made friends with minotaurs, furies, gorgons and chimeras. They were similarly disruptive and, I thought, similarly misunderstood. Then the busy world of Richard Scarry, everything Narnia related, books about frogs and dogs and plants that ate flies and anything Roald Dahl could think of. And for about a year, absolutely anything to do with stars and planets and the night sky. I threw myself into *Charlotte's Web* and cut my way out waving a Silver Sword.

The library became the cathedral where I would come to worship and the stories were as precious to me as prayers. As I grew older my tastes became more discriminate. Instead of trying to read everything I could, I sought out the books I heard the 'cool people' talking about. The teachers who I liked, programmes on the TV that sounded clever. Basically, all wonderful, and all extra-curricular. The library was my partner-in-crime. When I should have been reading Jane Austen, it aided and abetted me to read Sylvia Plath. We were naughty together, the library and me. I would show it my membership card and it would show me the world.

When I was a little older, maybe thirteen or fourteen and 'deep', there was a habit I picked up at Loughton Library that I would have still today, if the world were a less computerised place. At the back of each book used to be a slip of paper which had the date stamps, detailing all the times the books had been released into the wild. I remember in my early teens taking books from the shelves and only checking out those that had sat unread for five years or more. I did it because I couldn't bear the idea of any part of that place being neglected and unloved. In return the library took me on adventures that not even the 'cool people' could have warned me about. I went on obscure adventures up the Ganges river, learned the rituals of Hasidic Jews and got some way through the once extolled merits of electroshock therapy (I'm not really surprised that book didn't have much of a social life).

The library is a different one now, and I cannot claim to be as 'deep', but I love taking my son to our local. We choose our piles with great care and excitement. He's one and a half, and I am pleased to report that so far we have learned that Spot loves his mum and Spot loves his dad, and Caterpillars can be very hungry indeed. As can children, as long as libraries exist to feed them.

THE DEFENCE OF THE BOOK

Julian Barnes

From a proposed second edition of *England, England*

(As Sir Jack Pitman's project for a replica version of England on the Isle of Wight proves an enormous commercial success, the mainland, or 'Old England' as it has come to be known, goes into sharp decline . . .)

. . . The first signs had been misleading, and greeted by some islanders with delight. After Scotland and Wales had left the Union, and Northern Ireland been reunited with the Republic, Europe lost patience with the sulky rump that remained. Decades of carping from the sidelines, while constantly demanding special favours and the repatriation of powers, were finally repaid. Germany and France, strongly backed by Europe's newest Celtic adherents, led a swift campaign to evict England. 'At last', as the ninety-three-year-old European President-for-Life Angela Merkel put it, 'we are repatriating to you your powers, and not just the ones you asked for, but all the other ones as well.'

There was much excitement, as the country, having become smaller and less influential, had also become more xenophobic. The *Daily Mail* which, after the demise of *The Times*, was widely referred to as 'the newspaper of record', funded street parties and firework displays. But the euphoria was brief. Europe, not content just to evict England, also wanted to bring her low. Subtle and sometimes unsubtle trade barriers were raised; appeals to international organisations against such tariffs failed. The United States had long been looking westward, and now tended to regard England as an embarrassing ancestor, and a case for humane termination.

Trade collapsed, and the nation's infrastructure with it. The Health Service, long privatised, had become known to the poor as the Death Service, since the government was now only responsible for the minimal duty to dispose of dead bodies. For the few surviving rich, there were regular flights to the continent, from which they returned with new German hips, cataract-free Czech eyes, and all manner of French cosmetic enhancement. Pensions were no longer paid, and rubbish no longer collected. Looted and burnt-out shops were a common sight;

communities gated themselves in; armed guards protected allotments at night.

Poverty threw up a few improvements, like the renaissance of the canal system. The re-establishment of the old barter system was welcomed by many. But it was the Defence of the Book that caused the most surprise. The widespread library protests of the early 2010s, more than a generation back, meant that much of the service had then been saved, an outcome for which all three parties had taken the credit (though it was thought that the ritual suicides of three novelists and a poet outside the Houses of Parliament had proved the tipping point). But little opposition was expected when the National Coalition announced that every remaining library was to be closed within a month. Since the digitalisation of all forms of information, libraries – like churches under Communism – were inhabited mainly by the elderly, that last generation which held on to the idea of the physical book as an item of value in itself.

Since the contents of libraries were deemed valueless, the Coalition simply instructed its enforcement agency (formerly known as the Army) to burn the buildings to the ground. But after the first two incinerations, there were mass protests, and human shields were formed round many libraries. More menacingly, two offices of the enforcement agency were burnt down in retaliation. There was a broad suspicion, especially among the elderly, that once information and culture were only available digitally through the *englandwideweb*, truth would be easier for the government to control. To the surprise of many, the printed book began to take on a symbolic significance, as once it had done in the early years of printing.

This standoff continued for several months, because even to the National Coalition the notion of scores of incinerated citizens as acceptable collateral damage seemed a little excessive. There was negotiation; promises were made, and then more promises, until – to the government's surprise – the armies of white-haired activists agreed to stop protecting libraries in exchange for an official promise to keep them open, on terms and conditions to be mutually agreed. Naturally, as soon as the defendants withdrew, the government sent in its enforcers with the instruction that not a book survive. Indeed, there was a ministerial memo proposing that the very word 'book' should be withdrawn from public discourse. When the thing no longer existed, the word to denote it would surely not survive either.

But when the official arsonists arrived to carry out their work, they discovered that all the libraries had been secretly emptied of their contents. One by one, often at night, books had been removed to safety. At first they were simply hidden, in attics, hayricks and henhouses. And so the government concluded that it had in any case won: the book had gone into internal exile and would die off when those arm-linking old fools who had held up progress for the length of a summer died off themselves. Yet in this they were much deceived. The truth was only pieced together many decades later. But it seems that at first there was a samizdat circulation of individual books among trusted 'readers'. Then, in a bold move started in West Yorkshire, the first underground mobile library was set up by a book-loving milkman whose horse-drawn cart held a secret compartment in which a few dozen volumes could be hidden. Since books were scarce and forbidden by authority, children suddenly valued them the more. Boldly, adults began meeting in 'reading groups', which passed round a single existing copy of a book and then discussed it in its absence; many of these groups were raided but without success. Finally, books began to multiply, from which the only conclusion to be drawn was that an underground publishing and printing company had been set up. The government, for all its enforcement agencies, was unable to discover either the location or the membership of this enterprise.

Later, much later, this famous Defence of the Book was regularly compared by historians to the way in which culture and learning were kept alive by monks during the Dark Ages until better, safer times returned. And even if others maintained that this renaissance would have occurred anyway, it is nonetheless true that this Defence of the Book, both actual and symbolic, undoubtedly led to . . .

THE PUNK AND LANGSIDE LIBRARY

HARDEEP SINGH KOHLI

Punk. Even the word, with its harsh consonant beginning and even harsher consonant ending, filled me with a certain dread. (For younger readers, we are in 1981. While we may have had running water and electricity we had still to experience the colonisation of our language by the Americans. Back then, Punk had absolutely nothing to do with Ashton Kutcher. Or Clint Eastwood.)

The nihilism and anarchy of Punk was well documented; somehow it included random spitting, sculpted hair and safety pins. And also, amongst some Punks, there was a definite racist agenda. Understandably, it was this wing of Punk that most concerned my parents and me; not the early (non-racist) work of the Buzzcocks.

I was twelve years old. Glasgow was hard enough

work, given the sectarian divide and the confusion I caused by being a Sikh who openly attended a Catholic school. My bottle-green tie, blazer and turban combo nailed my school colours firmly to the mast. The last thing I needed was the introduction of Punks to Glasgow. Yet another potential kicking to run from.

And in terms of avoidance, I had done a pretty good job, up until that cold, dark, late November evening.

Langside Library was and continues to be a special place. It sits with prominence on Sinclair Drive, at the bottom of Battlefield Road, down the hill from the monument. Across the road is the Victoria Infirmary; in front of the beautiful sandstone house of books is a funny wee road set-up where the buses turn around, a terminus, a destination. Much like the library itself: a destination, where lives turn around.

Every day after school I'd walk down to my wee mum's shop. Sometimes I'd sit in the back and read magazines, carefully, before putting them back on the shelf. Sometimes I'd sit in the car and fall in love with Annie Nightingale on Radio 1. And sometimes I'd be told to go to Langside Library to do my homework.

I liked the library. The smell of books. The comfy chairs. The stern, matronly librarian who had more than the faintest whiff of lavender and/or travel sweets about her. My mum grew up with very few books around her. This inculcated her with a sense of reverence towards them, a reverence she passed on to her kids. So being around books made me feel almost spiritual at times. I would sit on a hard, vinyl-covered chair, at a table, under an unforgiving light; I would struggle with my work while my uber-bright younger brother would have sailed through all his assignments and repair to the cosseted comfort of the reclining chairs where he would tear through a book for pleasure.

One Wednesday almost thirty years ago I found myself racing the fading light of an oncoming Glasgow winter as I shuffled off to Langside Library. (The gloaming won). The comforting warmth of the library was most welcome. A collection of the usual faces, the usual whispered voices and hushed tones belied the unique and surprising events that were about to unfold.

There is a protocol in libraries; those of us that frequent them know how to move around the space noiselessly. We know the level at which to pitch a conversation when asking the staff for a copy of last year's 'oor wullie' annual. We know this. Alan the punk didn't.

The image will never leave me: a cockney punk in the leafier enclaves of Glasgow's Southside. Ripped tartan trousers, Doc Marten boots, spiky hair and a black leather biker's jacket. In Battlefield. Incongruity in action.

He removed books from shelves noisily; he strutted about noisily; he breathed noisily.

It seemed ironic that the fat, brown kid in the

bottle-green uniform and matching turban was, for once, not the strangest looking person around.

I knew that a clock was ticking. The lavender-smelling librarian would have to act, would be compelled to say something to the noisy punk. It was just a matter of time. I kept watching him from behind a biology textbook, waiting for the inevitable denouement.

The punk wandered over towards me. I was sure he would walk past. But he didn't.

'Oi, Paki. You got a light?' He spoke this in his normal voice. There was nothing *sotto voce* about it. For a moment I wasn't sure he was talking to me. The words seemed dislocated from their sense. I wasn't a Paki. Why did he need light?

'Oi. Paki. Have you got any matches?'

Then it became clear that I was the object of his attention.

'I'm not a Paki.' A fairly basic riposte, but factually correct. And he was a few years older and considerably taller than me. He had heard my accent which seemed at that point to cause him no end of entertainment.

'Scottie. You're a Scottie. That's funny . . .'

No one ever thought I was Scottish. It was always assumed that I was Indian; the brown skin a giveaway.

'Yes. I'm Scottish. And why's that funny?'

I have no idea where my bravery came from.

'Never met a Paki Scottie,' he said.

His English accent seemed to be twice as loud as

any other sound currently occurring in the universe at that point in time. And the librarian had heard it.

The details of the conversation that then took place are lost on me. All I know is that somehow I became inculcated in the act of anarchy caused by the punk. Me and the cockney punk found ourselves removed from the library after stern words. This joint ejection created an *esprit de corps* between us. We both felt wronged, but for very different reasons.

The punk was intent on smoking a cigarette. He decided that this could best be done in the trees around the library. We stood in the lea of the library and he managed to find a willing smoker to share some fire. And I stood and spoke to a punk. He was still hugely entertained by the notion that brown people could sound Scottish. And I was hugely surprised to realise that behind the spiked hair, torn tartan trousers and biker jacket resided a fairly pleasant guy, a guy who felt as misunderstood by the world as I did. He stopped calling me Paki and started calling me Scottie. We chatted for a bit. He lit his second cigarette from the dying embers of his first and, almost unthinkingly, handed it to me to have a drag. I was twelve. I didn't smoke. But somehow, in that moment, in that chance coming together of two disparate souls, I felt I couldn't let him down. I dragged on the cigarette. And coughed for a few moments. He found that hysterical.

We parted ways shortly thereafter, the last word he said to me was 'Scottie'. And I trudged back. In the fully-formed darkness to my mum's shop. And as I did, I thought about the library and how it had managed to let two such different people from two such different worlds collide. It took a visiting cockney punk to allow me, for the first time, to have my Scottishness expressed and accepted. And it happened in a library.

I spent a great deal of time after that in libraries, through school and university and since. To reduce a library to simple architecture, bricks and mortar is a mistake. Similarly, to suggest a library is defined by the books on the shelf is erroneous. Libraries are very special spaces, spaces where people come together in separate but joint pursuits of knowledge, of learning. Libraries are the heartbeats of communities.

A library was the place I met my first ever punk. A library was a place where I was able to claim my Scottishness. And a library was the first place I puffed on a fag. Two out of three ain't bad . . .

THE RULES

LUCY MANGAN

When life – or the government – gives you lemons, make lemonade, say I! Especially if you can't find a member of the Cabinet, rabbit-punch him to the ground and squeeze the lemons in his blank, soulless eyes.

The Big Society is here. And libraries aren't. If you can't see the opportunity here – well, then you aren't the irrepressible optimist I took you for.

I have, thanks to twenty years of more-or-less frenzied purchasing, more books than I can now read in a lifetime. The slowing heartbeat of print journalism could flatline any time and leave me bereft of job and purpose. The time has surely come to add a second string to my bow, and to give something back to my community, even if I have no idea who that community might actually be. But I'm sure you're out there, and if you ever see me waving, do say hello, won't you?

I'm going to start my own library. Both a borrower and a lender I'll be!

All I need is a rubber stamp, a few index cards and – in keeping with the idiosyncratic stock, which runs from Norah Lofts to Philip Roth via Narnia and includes not one but two biographies of Mary Pickford, which recent discovery did cause me to wonder whether I shouldn't hand over all my credit cards and financial decisions to my next of kin whenever I come within fifty miles of the Book Barn) – a handful of idiosyncratic rules. To wit:

1. All applicants for membership must provide a recently defaced picture of a cabinet minister, a packet of Tunnock's caramel wafers and a ten-minute go of a lovely kitten.

2. Silence is to be maintained at all times. For younger patrons, 'silence' is an ancient tradition, dating from pre-digital times. It means 'the absence of sound'. Sound includes talking. Such a state was thought to allow longer and deeper engagement with a task – here, 'reading' – and we are attempting to resurrect the custom. We'd probably have more luck resurrecting Etruscan haruspicy, but you've got to try.

3. I will provide tea and coffee at cost price, the descriptive terms for which will be limited to

'black', 'white', 'no/one/two/three sugars' and 'cup'. Anyone who asks for a latte, cappuccino or herbal anything will be taken outside and killed. Silently.

4. Opening hours are noon to midnight. I'm not a morning person.

5. There will be no food provided or permitted in the library. Less because I am concerned for the state of my books than because I am concerned for mine and other users' sanity if they have to hear you masticating.

6. That word was 'masticating'. If you thought it was something else, please stay away from this and any other library.

7. Please place mobile phones in the box provided. They may or may not be returned to you depending on whether or not I fancy upgrading my Nokia Average.

8. Patrons may be accompanied by kittens at any time, dogs by special arrangement, babies by very special arrangement, because they're not quiet and they bugger up mornings too.

9. Central heating settings shall be decided by a show of hands. In the event of a tie, votes of menopausal women shall count double.

10. Dog-ear my pages and I'll dog-ear you.

BAFFLED AT A BOOKCASE

ALAN BENNETT

I have always been happy in libraries, though without ever being entirely at ease there. A scene that seems to crop up regularly in plays that I have written has a character, often a young man, standing in front of a bookcase feeling baffled. He – and occasionally she – is overwhelmed by the amount of stuff that has been written and the ground to be covered. 'All these books. I'll never catch up,' wails the young Joe Orton in the film script of *Prick Up Your Ears*, and in *The Old Country* another young man reacts more dramatically, by hurling half the books to the floor. In *Me, I'm Afraid of Virginia Woolf* someone else gives vent to their frustration with literature by drawing breasts on a photograph of Virginia Woolf and kitting out E.M. Forster with a big cigar. Orton himself notoriously defaced library books before starting to write books himself. This resentment, which was, I suppose, somewhere mine, had to do with feeling shut out. A library, I used to feel, was like a cocktail party with everybody standing with their back to me; I could not find a way in.

The first library I did find my way into was the Armley Public Library in Leeds where a reader's ticket cost tuppence in 1940; not tuppence a time or even tuppence a year but just tuppence; that was all you ever had to pay. It was rather a distinguished building, put up in 1901, the architect Percy Robinson, and amazingly for Leeds, which is and always has been demolition crazy, it survives and is still used as a library, though whether it will survive the present troubles I don't like to think.

We would be there as a family, my mother and father, my brother and me, and it would be one of our regular weekly visits. I had learned to read quite early when I was five or six, by dint, it seemed to me then, of watching my brother read. We both of us read comics but whereas I was still on picture-based comics like the *Dandy* and the *Beano*, my brother, who was three years older, had graduated to the more text-based *Hotspur* and *Wizard*. Having finished my *Dandy* I would lie down on the carpet beside him and gaze at what he was reading, asking him questions about it and generally making a nuisance of myself. Then – and it seemed as instantaneous as this – one day his comic made sense and I could read. I'm sure it must have been more painstaking than this but not much more.

Having learned to read, other than comics, there was nothing in the house on which to practise my newly acquired skill. My parents were both readers and Dad took the periodical *John Bull*, the books they generally favoured literature of escape, tales of ordinary folk like themselves who had thrown it all up for a life of mild adventure, a smallholding on the Wolds, say, or an island sanctuary, with both of them fans of the naturalist R.M. Lockley. There were a few volumes of self-help in the house but the only non-library book of autobiography was *I Haven't Unpacked* by William Holt, who had got away from the dark, satanic mills by buying a horse and riding through England.

The Armley library was at the bottom of Wesley Road, the entrance up a flight of marble steps under open arches, through brass-railed swing doors panelled in stained glass which by 1941 was just beginning to buckle. Ahead was the Adults' Library, lofty, airy and inviting; to the right was the Junior Library, a low, dark room made darker by the books which, regardless of their contents, had been bound in heavy boards of black, brown or maroon embossed with the stamp of Leeds Public Libraries. This grim packaging was discouraging to a small boy who had just begun to read, though more discouraging still was the huge and ill-tempered, walrus-moustached British Legion commissionaire who was permanently installed there. The image of General Hindenburg, who was pictured on the stamps in my brother's album, he had lost one or other of his limbs in the trenches, but since he seldom moved from his chair and just shouted it was difficult to tell which.

Such veterans of the First War were much in evidence well into the 1950s. As a child one encountered them in parks, sitting on benches and in shelters playing dominoes, generally grumpy and with reason to be, the war having robbed them of their youth and often their health. The luckier and less disabled ones manned lifts or were posted at the doors of public buildings, a uniformed and bemedalled conciergerie who were more often than not unhelpful, making the most of whatever petty authority they were invested with. And so it was here, the commissionaire's only concern to maintain absolute silence, and not at all the companion and friend novice readers needed on this, the threshold of literature.

Of the books themselves I remember little. Henty was well represented and Captain Marryat, books which whenever I did manage to get into them only brought home to me that I was not an entirely satisfactory version of the genus boy. I suppose there must somewhere have been Enid Blyton, but since she too would have been backed in the same funereal but immensely serviceable boards she passed me by. As it was, the books I best remember reading there were the Dr Dolittle stories of Hugh Lofting, which were well represented and (an important consideration) of which there were always more. I think I knew even at six years old that a doctor who could talk to animals was fiction but at the same time I thought the setting of the stories, Puddleby-on-the-Marsh, was a real place set in historical time with the doctor (and Lofting's own illustrations of the doctor) having some foundation in fact. Shreds of this belief clung on because when, years later, having recorded some of Lofting's stories for the BBC, I met his son, I found I still had the feeling that his father had been not quite an ordinary mortal.

Other mysteries persisted. What, for instance, was a cat's meat man? I had never come across one. Was the meat *of* cats or *for* cats? We didn't have a cat and even if we had with Dad being a Co-op butcher it would have been well catered for. And again it was when I was reading the stories on the radio and happened to mention this mysterious personage in my diary in the *London Review of Books* that the small mystery was solved. A cat's meat man toured the streets (though not our street) with strips of meat suspended from a stick to be sold as pet food. One correspondent, her mother being out, remembered the stick of meat being put through the letterbox where she retrieved it from the doormat and, it being wartime, scoffed the lot.

In 1944, believing, as people in Leeds tended to do, that flying bombs or no flying bombs, things were better Down South, Dad threw up his job with the Co-op and we migrated to Guildford. It was a short-lived experiment and I don't remember ever finding the public library, but this was because a few doors down from the butcher's shop where Dad worked there was a little private library, costing 6d a week, which in the children's section had a whole run of Richmal Crompton's *William* books. I devoured them, reading practically one a day, happy in the knowledge that there would always be more. Years later when I first read Evelyn Waugh I had the same sense of discovery: here was a trove of books that was going to last. I wish I could say I felt the same about Dickens or Trollope or Proust even, but they seemed more of a labour than a prospect of delight.

The butcher for whom my dad worked also ran a horsemeat business, the meat strictly for non-human consumption and accordingly painted bright green. In his cattle truck Mr Banks would go out into the Surrey countryside to collect carcasses and sometimes, by dint of hanging around the lorry, I got to go with him. I would watch as the bloated cow or horse was winched on board and then we would drive to the slaughterhouse in Walnut Tree Close just by Guildford Station. While the carcass was dismembered I would sit in the corner absorbed in my latest *William* book. Richmal Crompton can seldom have been read in such grisly and uncongenial circumstances.

It wasn't long, though, before we ended up going

back to Leeds where we now lived in Headingley, with the local public library on North Lane, a visit to which could be combined with seeing the film at the Lounge cinema opposite. I went to Leeds Modern School, a state school at Lawnswood (and now called Lawnswood). I spoke there a few months ago and, unlike Ofsted, was much impressed by it, its current disfavour a presumed punishment for its admirable headmistress, who is still managing to resist the siren charms of academy status and the wiles of Mr Gove. In those circumstances I am happy to boast that the school library has been named after me.

When I was in the sixth form at the Modern School I used to do my homework in the Leeds Central Library in the Headrow. At that time the municipal buildings housed not only the lending library and the reference library but also the education offices and the police department, which I suppose was handy for the courts, still functioning across the road in the town hall with the whole complex – town hall, library, courts – an expression of the confidence of the city and its belief in the value of reading and education, and where you might end up if they were neglected. It's a High Victorian building done throughout in polished Burmantofts brick, extravagantly tiled, the staircases of polished marble topped with brass rails, and carved at the head of each stair a slavering dog looking as if it's trying to stop itself sliding backwards down the banister.

Armley Public Library

The reference library itself proclaimed the substance of the city with its solid elbow chairs and long mahogany tables, grooved along the edge to hold a pen, and in the centre of each table a massive pewter inkwell. Arched and galleried and lined from floor to ceiling with books, the reference library was grand yet unintimidating. Half the tables were filled with sixth-formers like myself, just doing their homework or studying for a scholarship; but there would also be university students home for the vacation, the Leeds students tending to work up the road in their own Brotherton Library. There were, too, the usual quota of eccentrics that haunt any reading room that is warm and handy and has somewhere to sit down. Old men would doze for hours over a magazine taken from the rack, though if they were caught nodding off an assistant would trip over from the counter and hiss, 'No sleeping!'

One regular, always with a pile of art books at his elbow, was the painter Jacob Kramer, some of whose paintings, with their Vorticist slant, hung in the art gallery next door. Dirty and half-tight there wasn't much to distinguish him from the other tramps whiling away their time before trailing along Victoria Street to spend the night in the refuge in the basement of St George's Church, where occasionally I would do night duty myself, sleeping on a camp bed in a room full of these sad, defeated, utterly unthreatening creatures.

With its mixture of readers and its excellent facilities (it was a first-rate library) and the knowledge that there would always be someone working there whom I knew and who would come out for coffee, I found some of the pleasure in going to the reference library that, had I been less studious, I could have found in a pub. Over the next ten years while I still thought I might turn into a medieval historian I became something of a connoisseur of libraries, but the reference library in Leeds always seemed to me one of the most congenial. It was there, on leave from the army, that I discovered they held a run of *Horizon*, the literary magazine started by Cyril Connolly in 1940, and that I eventually did get a scholarship to Oxford I put down to the smattering of culture I gleaned from its pages.

In my day, it was a predominantly male institution with the main tables dividing themselves almost on religious or ethnic lines. There was a Catholic table, patronised by boys from St Michael's College, the leading Catholic school, with blazers in bright Mary blue; there was a Jewish table where the boys came from Roundhay or the Grammar School, the Jewish boys even when they were not at the same school often knowing each other from the synagogue or other extra-curricular activities. If, like me, you were at the Modern School – and there were about half a dozen of us who were there regularly – you had no particular religious or racial affinities and indeed were not thought perhaps quite as clever, the school certainly not as good as Roundhay or the Grammar School. The few girls who braved this male citadel disrupted the formal division, leavened it, I'm sure for the better. And they worked harder than the boys and were seldom to be found on the landing outside where one adjourned for a smoke.

It had glamour, too, for me and getting in first at nine one morning I felt, opening my books, as I had when a small boy at Armley Baths and I had been first in there, the one to whom it fell to break the immaculate stillness of the water, shatter the straight lines tiled on the bottom of the bath and set the day on its way.

Of the boys who worked in the reference library a surprising number must have turned out to be lawyers, and I can count at least eight of my contemporaries who sat at those tables in the 1950s who became judges. A school – and certainly a state or provincial school – would consider that something to boast about, but libraries are facilities; a library has no honours board and takes no credit for what its readers go on to do but, remembering myself at nineteen, on leave from the army and calling up the copies of *Horizon* to get me through the general paper in the Oxford scholarship, I feel as much a debt to that library as I do to my school. It was a good library and though like everywhere else busier now than it was in my day, remains, unlike so much of Leeds, largely unaltered.

The library closed at nine and coming down in the lift (bevelled mirrors, mahogany panelling, little bench) the attendant, another British Legion figure, would stop and draw the gates at the floor below and in would get a covey of policemen and even the occasional miscreant en route for the cells. One of the policemen might be my cousin Arnold, who belonged to what my mother always felt was the slightly common wing of the Bennett family. Loud, burly and wonderfully genial, Arnold was a police photographer and he would regale me with the details of the latest murder he had been called on to snap: 'By, Alan, I've seen some stuff.' The stuff he'd seen included the corpse of the stripper Mary Millington, who had committed suicide. 'I can't understand why she committed suicide. She had a lovely body.'

To someone as prone to embarrassment as I was,

these encounters, particularly in the presence of my schoolfriends, ought to have been shaming. That they never were was, I suppose, because Cousin Arnold was looked on as a creature from the real world, the world of prostitutes found dead on waste ground, corpses in copses and cars burned out down Lovers' Lane. This was Life where I knew even then that I was not likely to be headed or ever to have much to do with.

There is no shortage of libraries in Oxford, some of them, of course, of great grandeur and beauty. The Radcliffe Camera seems to me one of the handsomest buildings in England and the square in which it stands a superb combination of styles. Crossing it on a moonlit winter's night lifted the heart, though that was often the trouble with Oxford – the architecture out-soared one's feelings, the sublime not always easy to match. There are in that one square three libraries, the Bodleian on the north side, on the east the Codrington, part of Hawksmoor's All Souls, and James Gibbs's Camera in the middle. There is actually another more modest library, neo-Gothic in style, and built by George Gilbert Scott in 1856. It's over Exeter's garden wall in the north-west corner of Radcliffe Square, but you can't quite see that. This was where I worked, though it was possible if one was so inclined to get to study in the much more exclusive and architecturally splendid surroundings of the Codrington, and a few undergraduates did so. They tended, though, to set less store on what they were writing than on where they were writing it and I, with my narrow sympathies but who was just as foolish, despised them for it.

Staying on at Oxford after I'd taken my degree I did research in medieval history, the subject of my research Richard II's retinue in the last ten years of his reign. This took me twice a week to the Public Record Office then still in Chancery Lane and in particular to the Round Room, galleried, lined with books, a humbler version of the much grander Round Room in the British Museum. Presiding over the BM Round Room in his early days was Angus Wilson whereas at the PRO it was Noel Blakiston, friend of Cyril Connolly, hair as white as Wilson's and possibly the most distinguished-looking man I've ever seen.

Though I made copious notes on the manuscripts I studied (which were chiefly records of the medieval exchequer) I would have found it hard to say what it was I was looking for – imagining, I think, that having amassed sufficient material it would all suddenly fall into place and become clear. Failing that, I hoped to come upon some startling and unexpected fact, a very silly notion. Had it been Richard III I was researching rather than Richard II, it might have been something as relatively unambiguous as a note in the monarch's own hand saying: 'It was me that killed ye Princes in ye Tower, hee hee.' Historical research nowadays is a dull business: had I any sense I would have been collating the tax returns of the knights I was studying or the amount they borrowed or were owed, or sifting through material other historians had ignored or discarded; it is seldom at the frontier that discoveries are made but more often in the dustbin.

The Memoranda Rolls on which I spent much of my time were long thin swatches of parchment about five feet long and one foot wide and written on both sides. Thus to turn the page required the co-operation and forbearance of most of the other readers at the table, and what would sometimes look like the cast of the Mad Hatter's tea party struggling to put wallpaper up was just me trying to turn over. A side-effect of reading these unwieldy documents was that one was straightaway propelled into quite an intimate relationship with readers alongside and among those I got to know in this way was the historian Cecil Woodham-Smith.

The author of *The Great Hunger*, an account of the Irish Famine, and *The Reason Why*, about the events leading up to the Charge of the Light Brigade, Cecil was a frail woman with a tiny bird-like skull, looking more like Elizabeth I (in later life) than Edith Sitwell ever did (and minus her sheet metal earrings). Irish, she had a Firbankian wit and a lovely turn of phrase. 'Do you know the Atlantic at all?' she once asked me and I put the line into *Habeas Corpus* and got a big laugh on it. From a grand Irish family, she was quite snobbish; talking of someone she said: 'Then he married a Mitford . . . but that's a stage everybody goes through.' Even the most ordinary remark would be given her own particular twist and she could be quite camp. Conversation had once turned, as conversations will, to fork-lift trucks. Feeling that industrial machinery might be remote from Cecil's sphere of interest I said: 'Do you know what a fork-lift truck is?' She looked at me in her best Annie Walker manner. 'I do. To my cost.'

Books and bookcases cropping up in stuff that I've written means that they have to be reproduced on stage or on film. This isn't as straightforward as it might seem. A designer will either present you with shelves lined with gilt-tooled library sets, the sort of clubland books one can rent by the yard as decor, or he or she will send out for some junk books from the nearest second-hand bookshop and think that those will do. Another short cut is to order in a cargo of remaindered books so that you end up with a shelf so garish and lacking in character it bears about as much of a relationship to literature as a caravan site does to architecture. A bookshelf is as particular to its owner as are his or her clothes; a personality is stamped on a library just as a shoe is shaped by the foot.

That someone's working library has a particular tone, with some shelves more heterogeneous than others, for example, or (in the case of an art historian) filled with offprints and monographs or (with an old-fashioned literary figure, for instance) lined with the faded covers and jackets of distinctive Faber or Cape editions, does not seem to occur to a designer. On several occasions I've had to bring my own books down to the theatre to give the right worn tone to the shelves.

In *The Old Country* (1977) the books (Auden, Spender, MacNeice) are of central importance to the plot. I wanted their faded buffs and blues and yellows bleached into a unity of tone that suggested long sunlit Cambridge afternoons, the kind of books you might find lining Dadie Rylands's rooms, for instance. Anthony Blunt's bookshelves were crucial in *Single Spies*, the look of an art historian's bookshelves significantly different from those of a literary critic say. All this tends to pass the designer by. One knows that designers seldom read, but they don't have much knowledge of Inca civilisation either or the Puritan settlement of New England and yet they seem to cope perfectly well reproducing them. An agglomeration of books as illustrating the character of their owner seems to defeat them.

When I first bought books for myself in the late 1940s they were still thought to be quite precious and in poor homes books might often be backed in brown paper. Paper itself was in short supply and such new books as there were often bore the imprint 'Produced in conformity with the Authorised Economy Standard'. The paper was mealy, slightly freckled and looked not unlike the texture of the ice cream of the period. It was, though, a notable period in book design and perhaps because they were among the first books I ever bought (one was C.V.

Wedgwood's *William the Silent*) the books of that time have always seemed to me all that was necessary or desirable – simple, unfussy, wholesome and well designed.

They were not, though, to be left about at home. 'Books Do Furnish a Room', wrote Anthony Powell, but my mother never thought so and she'd always put them out of the way in the sideboard when you weren't looking. Books untidy, books upset, more her view. Though once a keen reader herself, particularly when she was younger, she always thought of library books as grubby and with a potential for infection – not intellectual infection either. Lurking among the municipally owned pages might be the germs of TB or scarlet fever, so one must never be seen to peer at a library book too closely or lick your finger before turning over, still less read such a book in bed.

There were other perils to reading, but it was only when I hit middle age that I became aware of them. *Me, I'm Afraid of Virginia Woolf* was a television play written in 1978 and though it doesn't contain my usual scene of someone baffled at a bookcase the sense of being outfaced by books is a good description of what the play is about. 'Hopkins,' I wrote of the middle-aged lecturer who is the hero, 'Hopkins was never without a book. It wasn't that he was particularly fond of reading; he just liked to have somewhere to look. A book makes you safe. Shows you're not out to pick anybody up. Try it on. With a book you're harmless. Though Hopkins was harmless without a book.' Books as badges, books as shields; one doesn't think of libraries as perilous places where you can come to harm. Still, they do carry their own risks.

I have been discussing libraries as places and in the current struggle to preserve public libraries not enough stress has been laid on the library as a place, not just a facility. To a child living in high flats, say, where space is at a premium and peace and quiet not always easy to find, a library is a haven. But, saying that, a library needs to be handy and local; it shouldn't require an expedition. Municipal authorities of all parties point to splendid new and scheduled central libraries as if this discharges them of their obligations. It doesn't. For a child a library needs to be round the corner. And if we lose local libraries it is children who will suffer. Of the libraries I have mentioned the most important for me was that first one, the dark and unprepossessing Armley Junior Library. I had just learned to read. I needed books. Add computers to that requirement maybe but a child from a poor family is today in exactly the same boat.

The business of closing libraries isn't a straightforward political fight. The local authorities shelter behind the demands of central government which in its turn pretends that local councils have a choice. It's shaming that, regardless of the party's proud tradition of popular education, Labour municipalities are not making more of a stand. For

the Tories privatising the libraries has been on the
agenda for far longer than they would currently like
to admit. This is an extract from my diary:

22 *February* Switch on *Newsnight* to find some
bright spark from, guess where, the Adam Smith
Institute, proposing the privatisation of the public
libraries. His name is Eamonn Butler and it's to be
hoped he's no relation of the 1944 Education Act
Butler. Smirking and pleased with himself as they
generally are from that stable, he's pitted against
a well-meaning but flustered woman who's an
authority on children's books. Paxman looks on
undissenting as this odious figure dismisses any
defence of the tradition of free public libraries as
'the usual bleating of the middle classes'. I go to bed
depressed only to wake and find Madsen Pirie, also
from the Adam Smith Institute for the Criminally
Insane, banging the same drum in the *Independent*.
Not long ago John Bird and John Fortune did a
sketch about the privatisation of air. These days it
scarcely seems unthinkable.

That was written in 1996. It's hard not to think that
like other Tory policies privatising the libraries has
been lying dormant for fifteen years, just waiting for
a convenient crisis to smuggle it through. Libraries
are, after all, as another think-tank clown opined a
few weeks ago, 'a valuable retail outlet'.

THE FUTURE OF THE LIBRARY

SETH GODIN

What is a public library for?

First, how we got here.

Before Gutenberg, a book cost about as much as a small house. As a result, only kings and bishops could afford to own a book of their own.

This naturally led to the creation of shared books, of libraries where scholars (everyone else was too busy not starving) could come to read books that they didn't have to own. *The library as warehouse for books worth sharing.*

Only after that did we invent the librarian.

The librarian isn't a clerk who happens to work at a library. A librarian is a data hound, a guide, a sherpa and a teacher. The librarian is the interface between reams of data and the untrained but motivated user.

After Gutenberg, books got a lot cheaper. More individuals built their own collections. At the same time, though, the number of titles exploded, and the demand for libraries did as well. We definitely needed a warehouse to store all this bounty, and more than ever we needed a librarian to help us find what we needed. *The library is a house for the librarian.*

Industrialists (particularly Andrew Carnegie) funded the modern American library. The idea was that in a pre-electronic media age, the working man needed to be both entertained and slightly educated. Work all day and become a more civilised member of society by reading at night.

And your kids? Your kids need a place with shared encyclopedias and plenty of fun books, hopefully inculcating a lifelong love of reading, because reading makes all of us more thoughtful, better informed and more productive members of a civil society.

Which was all great, until now.

Want to watch a movie? Netflix is a better librarian, with a better library, than any library in the country. The Netflix librarian knows about every movie, knows what you've seen and what you're likely to want to see. If the goal is to connect viewers with movies, Netflix wins.

This goes further than a mere sideline that most librarians resented anyway. Wikipedia and the huge databanks of information have basically eliminated the library as the best resource for anyone doing amateur research (grade school, middle school, even undergrad). Is there any doubt that online resources will get better and cheaper as the years go by? Kids don't schlep to the library to use an out-of-date encyclopedia to do a report on FDR. You might want them to, but they won't unless coerced.

They need a librarian more than ever (to figure out creative ways to find and use data). They need a library not at all.

When kids go to the mall instead of the library, it's not that the mall won, it's that the library lost.

And then we need to consider the rise of the Kindle. An e-book costs about $1.60 in 1962 dollars. A thousand ebooks can fit on one device, easily. Easy to store, easy to sort, easy to hand to your neighbour. Five years from now, readers will be as expensive as Gillette razors, and ebooks will cost less than the blades.

Librarians who are arguing and lobbying for clever ebook lending solutions are completely missing the point. They are defending library as warehouse as opposed to fighting for the future, which is librarian as producer, concierge, connector, teacher and impresario.

Post-Gutenberg, books are finally abundant, hardly scarce, hardly expensive, hardly worth warehousing. Post-Gutenberg, the scarce resource is knowledge and insight, not access to data.

The library is no longer a warehouse for dead books. Just in time for the information economy, the library ought to be the local nerve centre for information. (Please don't say I'm anti-book! I think through my actions and career choices, I've demonstrated my pro-book chops. I'm not saying I *want* paper to go away, I'm merely describing what's inevitably occurring.) We all love the vision of the underprivileged kid bootstrapping himself out of poverty with books, but now (most of the time), the insight and leverage is going to come from being fast and smart with online resources, not from hiding in the stacks.

The next library is a place, still. A place where people come together to do co-working and coordinate and invent projects worth working on together. Aided by a librarian who can bring domain knowledge and people knowledge and access to information to bear.

The next library is a house for the librarian with the guts to invite kids in to teach them how to get better grades while doing less grunt work. And to teach them how to use a soldering iron or take apart something with no user serviceable parts inside. And even to challenge them to teach classes on their passions, merely because it's fun. This librarian takes responsibility/blame for any kid who manages to graduate from school without being a first-rate data shark.

The next library is filled with so many web terminals there's always at least one empty. And the people who run this library don't view the combination of access to data and connections to peers as a sidelight – it's the entire point.

Wouldn't you want to live and work and pay taxes in a town that had a library like that? The vibe of the best Brooklyn coffee shop combined with a passionate raconteur of information? There are one thousand things that could be done in a place like this, all built around one mission: *take the world of data, combine it with the people in this community and create value.*

We need librarians more than we ever did. What we don't need are mere clerks who guard dead paper. Librarians are too important to be a dwindling voice in our culture. For the right librarian, this is the chance of a lifetime.

GOING TO THE DOGS

Val McDermid

I would not be a writer if it were not for the public library system. Books were a luxury we couldn't afford when I was growing up, but the working-class culture of my time and place was that education was the way you escaped your history. And education came courtesy of books.

My mother used to take me to the public library to look at picture books years before I could read. She would find a quiet corner of the children's section and tell me the stories, pointing out the pictures. I couldn't even pronounce the word – I used to say we were going to the Labrador. My mother says I've been going to the dogs ever since.

When I was six years old, we moved house. My parents couldn't have chosen a better location as far as I was concerned. Our new house was right across the road from the imposing sandstone building that still houses Kirkcaldy Central Library. The other half of the classically styled self-improvement centre is the Museum and Art Gallery, which is home to an impressive collection of Scottish Colourists. The whole thing was the gift of one of the linoleum manufacturers who got rich on the hard graft of their workers. I'm not sure whether this municipal munificence was a thank-you or a means of keeping us out of trouble. Either way, I welcomed it.

The library became my home from home. Its image is as clear in my mind's eye as the reality was at the time. High ceilings, cream paint, wood panelling and shelves stained a shade that usually appears on colour charts as 'antique pine'. The room was divided by waist-high wooden walls, with a wooden swing gate on either side of the central issuing desk. On one side lay the books for borrowing. On the other, long tables with hard chairs where, until closing time at 6.45, you could read the reference collection and the handful of worthy magazines the library subscribed to. There were no comics. Of course there were no comics. Libraries were for self-improvement, not frivolity.

To get into the section with the books, you had to have a library ticket. If you didn't have a ticket and you weren't returning a book, the librarian wouldn't let you in. It was simple.

I read voraciously, diving into the worlds of other people's imagination and emerging with my own vision enriched and inflamed. I could happily get through two books in a day. I read everywhere. At the table, in the street, in bed, at break time in school. Once I gave myself a black eye by walking into a castellated garden wall during my paper round while I was busily poring over the hockey reports in *The Scotsman*.

I read all of Enid Blyton except for the Secret Seven, who irritated me for some reason. I read *Just William, Jennings and Darbishire* and *Biggles*. I adored the Chalet School series and dreamed of being sent to an Alpine boarding school. I worked my way through the Bobbsey Twins, the Hardy Boys and Nancy Drew, and coveted her little red roadster. I read the Moomintrolls and *Worzel Gummidge* and Robert Louis Stevenson. I read *The Secret Garden* and *Oliver Twist*. Even though I was on the plump side myself, I read *Billy Bunter*.

My big problem always came at weekends. I used to spend part of my weekends and school holidays with my grandparents in a nearby mining village that had no library. And although we were allowed to take out four books at a time, two of them had to be non-fiction. After all, this was Presbyterian Scotland in the 1960s. Heaven forfend we should have unmitigated pleasure.

I did my best. I worked my way through poetry and drama, natural history and history. I even gritted my teeth and read some of the geography and travel section. But a lot of it was dry as dust or else incomprehensible. So more often than not, I ended up at my grandparents' house in a state of intense frustration at not having anything to read other than the two novels I'd just finished.

My grandparents were not readers. They had a copy of the Bible, because back then everybody did. But I had enough of the Bible at Sunday School, and besides, it was hard to pick out the good bits from the begats. They only had one other book in the house, which I've always assumed a visitor left behind. It was *The Murder at the Vicarage*, by Agatha Christie in the old Fontana edition, featuring an old-fashioned telephone with separate ear-piece and speaking trumpet.

It was love at first sight. And I suspect it stamped its influence on me for life.

Linguistic experts tell us Christie's prose can be read by anyone with a reading age of nine, and I was certainly a precocious reader, so I was probably working my way through it by the time I was seven or eight. I was captivated by it. This was the first Miss Marple, Christie at the peak of her powers. The plot is complicated by sub-plots and red herrings, and even though I knew after the first reading how the mystery was resolved, the book still retained its power to fascinate me.

What was almost more exciting was that there was a list of other books that Christie had written. I was desperate to read more. But now I came up against an insurmountable problem. Agatha Christie's books were not for children. They were in the adult library.

They might as well have been on Mars.

Some of the librarians were frankly terrifying, but others were friendly and helpful. But there was no way that even the kindest of them was going to let me loose in the adult library. I'm not sure what they thought might happen if a child wandered willy-nilly through the adult fiction, but they were not going to chance it.

I puzzled over this for a while. Then it dawned on me that compassion might succeed where all else failed. Early one morning, before my parents were awake, I opened the drawer where my mother kept her rarely used library tickets and helped myself to one. That evening, I turned up at the library and chose my own books. Then I went through to the admissions counter of the adult library. I put my mother's ticket on the counter and looked as piteous as I can manage.

'My mum's not well,' I said. 'I've to get her a book.'

My luck was in. The librarian on duty was not one of the dragons. She frowned and consulted one of her colleagues. They looked at the ticket and then looked back at me. 'That's fine,' she said, handing the ticket back.

The adult library was awesome. Fiction stretched all the way round the outer walls, with the non-fiction shelved on free-standing units in the middle. To either side was an impressive card index, one for fiction and one for non-fiction.

I made a beeline for Agatha Christie and found three of her books with the distinctive colophon of a masked gunman that marked the Collins Crime list. It was the start of a journey I'm still making through the genre I love. From Christie, my reading spread tree-like through classic British crime fiction. Conan Doyle, Allingham, Sayers, Ngaio Marsh and Michael Innes led me to contemporary writers such as Ruth Rendell and P.D. James. My English teacher pointed me at Raymond Chandler, which opened up another raft of writers to savour. I plundered the library, and when it couldn't satisfy my appetites, I came home with armfuls of scabby paperbacks from jumble sales and second-hand bookshops.

Being a reader turned me into a writer. It fed my imagination and revealed worlds far beyond my own experience. When I took the mighty leap in the dark to abandon my well-paid and secure job and attempt to make a living as a writer, I was too poor to afford books or music, and again it was the library that saved me. When I was starting to make my way as a writer, it was the support of librarians that helped me gain a readership.

Now I am a mother myself, I am proud to say my son also takes pleasure in libraries. Of course, his experience is rather different from mine. Open shelves beckon children to explore where they will. Almost unlimited borrowing allows them to read as much as they want to. And these days, author events give readers the chance to interact with their favourite authors in a way I'd have loved as a child.

Of course, sometimes author events do have their downside. A few years ago, I was invited back to Kirkcaldy Library. To my surprise, a couple of the librarians were still around from when I was younger. My mother, who still lives across from the library, is in her eighties now, but she had come to the event with me. I introduced her to the librarians. One seemed taken aback.

'Oh, Mrs McDermid,' she said, the words tumbling out before she thought better of them. 'I thought you must be dead by now.'

'Dead?' My mother sounded outraged. 'Why would I be dead?'

'Well, with you being a bed-ridden invalid all those years . . .' Her voice trailed off as she caught the look my mother cast my way.

Never mind. I still love libraries. And I'm still going to the dogs.

I ♥ LIBRARIES

LIONEL SHRIVER

One of my earliest memories from Raleigh, North Carolina, is of being led by my mother's hand into an awesomely big building downtown (it was doubtless very small) to acquire my first library card. Let loose in my personal version of a sweet shop, I scurried about amassing a stack of treats – *Curious George Goes to School*, *Where the Wild Things Are*, *Bartholomew and the Oobleck*. We were a frugal family, and these books were all for free!

Thus the campaign launched last month by a public–private partnership of publishers, library organisations, and the Department for Culture is wasted on me: 'Love Libraries'? I already do.

In some respects, this is admission against interest. As an author, I make much more money when you buy one of my books; if you borrow one from a library,

I make 3p. Still, I'll happily take the 3p. (Indeed, in the US writers enjoy no equivalent of Public Lending Rights, and I consider earning anything at all from borrowing perfectly fabulous.) For readers – and I myself read loads more books than I write – libraries offer a host of advantages over a bookstore.

When you've bought a book, you feel obligated to finish it, just to get your money's worth. But when I borrow the adult equivalent of that *Curious George* trove, I'm free to start a disappointing novel and discard it. Paying nothing for the book itself, I can place a higher premium on my time. The quality of the books that I do finish tends to rise.

In most bookstores, too, salespeople will look at you askance when you sprawl in the aisles with the new Ian McEwan. Libraries provide chairs, in which you can loll around reading *Saturday*, unharassed, for hours.

Yet for authors as well, libraries are invaluable. Unless it's a bestseller, the average hardback is likely to remain on bookstore shelves for about six weeks. With luck, perhaps a year later the paperback version will hit the stands; nevertheless, all but the most commercially successful paperbacks soon disappear as well. Without permanent acquisition by libraries, the fruit of many years' work simply vanishes from the cultural canon.

Publishers are increasingly resistant to keeping backlists in print. Since my seventh novel has (for once) sold pretty well, I am often approached by readers asking where they can buy the other six. Save one, they are all out of print, and flat-out unavailable at Waterstones. Though I sometimes direct punters to the internet, the cost of the few remaining copies of my older novels on Amazon is now soaring into hundreds of pounds per volume. Where are you most likely to find my previous titles, and at no cost whatsoever? *The library*. In fact, it is increasingly the case that a library is the only place you can find those books, no matter how rich you are, and many other authors' fine, but perhaps not *Da Vinci Code*-popular, books as well.

As a writer, I've also been able to avail myself of the extended services that contemporary libraries offer, including personal appearances that put me in touch with my readership and they with me. Library-sponsored book groups have fostered reading in general, which is great for writers.

So I owe libraries a debt – one that I hope someday to repay.

A little observed knock-on effect of Europe's low birth rate is that many people like me, who've had no children, will have no kids to whom to pass on their accumulated wealth when they die. I'm just old enough to start feeling a little weird about what happens to the property if, say, I buy a house. When I kick the bucket, does David Cameron move in? With so many childless couples in my generation and the ones behind me, I predict that in about twenty-five years a wave of charitable giving will start pouring into non-profit coffers from dead old people with no kids – along with massive state confiscation of orphaned assets when folks with neither children nor foresight die intestate.

Well, I'm not about to leave my worldly chattel to Dave, or whatever wasteful, avaricious bureaucrat replaces him, just to fund another catastrophic fiasco like Iraq. At the same time, I appreciate how hard it is to give away money well. I have four cousins whose lives have been virtually ruined by trust funds. I've lived in Africa, and witnessed firsthand how perversely destructive aid hand-outs can be; they skew local economies, feed government corruption, and undermine individual initiative. With shockingly high frequency, throwing money at people backfires.

So I've wracked my brains for somewhere to will my assets, using the physician's guideline, *First, do no harm*. I'm not about to repeat the mistake of my great-grandfather-by-marriage, and wreck the lives of my nieces and nephews with money that they didn't earn. After spending that year in Nairobi, I cannot conscionably support organisations that give aid to Africa, however well intentioned they may be. Then it hit me. Not only would the idea naturally suit a lifelong reader and writer, but what could possibly go wrong with a gift to *libraries*? How could you spoil anyone's life because they had access to free books? Or, to be more up to date, because they had access to the internet and computers, or were able to borrow CDs and DVDs for a pittance?

I am bequeathing whatever modest estate I accumulate by my death to the Belfast Library Board. For many penurious years, the little library on the Lisburn Road kept me reading wonderful books at a time that I couldn't afford to buy them. Often one of the first institutions to suffer cutbacks when public monies run short, libraries these days are woefully underfunded. So if by any chance I kick off a trend among the aging 'childfree', brilliant.

Meantime, just try sauntering into a WHSmith, shoving several books from the shelves into your rucksack, and waltzing past security with a promise that you'll bring them back.

HAVE YOU HEARD OF OSCAR WILDE?

STEPHEN FRY

I grew up in the country, deep in the country. The nearest major library was a twelve-mile bicycle ride into the city of Norwich. I was lucky to live in a house filled with books and to have parents who loved to read, but by the time I approached teenage my appetite for reading, combined with my more or less chronic insomnia, meant that I needed more, far more books to consume daily. Every other Thursday, a mobile library (in the form of a large grey pantechnicon that would today look absurdly old-fashioned) would come along and park not five minutes' walk from our house. This was my lifeline to the outside world. A quaint battleship-grey modem that linked me to the huge past and present that seemed so impossibly far from the lanes of rural Norfolk.

Aged eleven, one Saturday afternoon I sat in front

of our little black and white television set (despite the glowering disapproval of my father who thought – quite rightly of course – that television was a vulgar and despicable thing and that no healthy child should watch it, especially during the hours of sunlight) and watched breathless with enthralled disbelief as they screened a film directed by Anthony 'Puffin' Asquith. It was called *The Importance of Being Earnest* and it left me simply boggling with excitement. I had never heard language used in such a way, had never known that the rhythms of a sentence could be so beautiful, that meanings could turn with such wit on the hinge of a 'but' or an 'unless' – in short I had never known that writing could do more than tell a story, that it could *excite* in the way that music does. I remembered whole lines of dialogue and repeated them: phrases like 'I hope, Cecily, I shall not offend you if I state quite frankly and openly that you seem to me to be in every way the visible personification of absolute perfection' and 'some aunts are tall, some aunts are not tall. That is a matter that surely an aunt may be allowed to decide for herself.' I hugged these to me as I watched the credits roll by and memorised a name.

The following Thursday I ran to the corner of the lane and threw myself inside the mobile library the moment the door at the rear had opened and the steps been let down. 'Have you heard of Oscar Wilde?' I squealed to the cardiganed librarian within who clutched her beads in alarm at the urgency and intensity of my attack. 'Goodness me, young man . . .' 'Do you have a play he wrote called *The Importance of Being Earnest*?' 'Well now . . .' 'Please, I have to read it!'After what seemed an age we found a copy which was duly stamped. I ran home and up the stairs and into my bedroom.

I read *The Importance of Being Earnest* three or four times a day every day for two weeks. Then I returned it. I knew the whole play off by heart and can still distress companions with long quotations from it. 'What else do you have by Oscar Wilde?' I wanted to know. It was a different librarian and she found me a copy of the *Complete Works*.

Two weeks later I was back to have it restamped. I had read it from cover to cover, but I wanted to read it all again and again.

Another Library Thursday came and I reluctantly returned the *Complete Works* and asked if there was anything else by Oscar Wilde I could read. 'The *Complete Works* means the complete works,' the librarian explained. 'Oh but there must be something else . . .' The librarian gave a sigh and then looked me up and down. 'I'm not sure . . . but there is . . .' 'Yes? Yes?' She walked along the central corridor of the van and stooped low in the biography section . . . her face was flushed as she straightened and placed a book uncertainly into my hands. 'I really don't know if . . . how old are you, young man?' 'Thirteen,' I lied. It was an age that seemed impossibly mature. 'Well . . .' The book was called *The Trials of Oscar*

Wilde and was written by someone called H. Montgomery Hyde.

I took it home and read it. It was a book that changed my life. The heroic lord of language who had captivated me so entirely turned out to have had a secret life. And the more I read the faster my heart beat. For I knew that I shared the same secret. I had never quite dared tell myself this truth but reading of Wilde's arrest and trial I could not but know it to be true.

It was shattering, terrible, liberating, stimulating, appalling, wonderful and incredible all at once.

The mobile library a fortnight later had nothing more to offer so the following morning I caught a little motor coach early in the morning and went to Norwich. There in Esperanto Way stood the city's great library, since burned in a fire and replaced by a fine new one complete with cafés and all kinds of modern excitements.

It was here that I discovered how one book could lead one to another. Bibiliographies and footnotes suggested new names, new books, new writers, whole new areas to be discovered. It was an analogue, card-indexed way of mouse-clicking from one link to another. A little more laborious perhaps, but breathlessly exciting.

Over the next few years the trial and trail of Oscar had led me to read Gide and Genet, Auden and Orton, Norman Douglas and Ronald Firbank. Unforgettable, transformative books for me were that same H. Montgomery Hyde's *The Other Love*, Roger Peyrefitte's *The Exile of Capri* and *Special Friendships*, Angus Stewart's *Sandel* and Michael Campbell's *Lord Dismiss Us*. I read of man-love, boy-love and free love. I clutched to myself the dark secrets of the infamous Book 13 of the *Greek Anthology* and the Venice letters in *Quest for Corvo*. I read Cuthbert Worsley's *Flannelled Fool* and Robin Maugham's *Escape from the Shadows*. From over the Atlantic I encountered Gore Vidal and John Rechy. I discovered the Tangier set, by way of Michael Davies, Paul Bowles, William Burroughs and dozens of others.

For a gay youth growing up in the early '70s a library was a way of showing that I was not alone. There was an element of titillation and breath-taking possibility, even the chance of a fumbled encounter, but there was vindication too. Some of the best, finest, truest, cleverest minds that ever held a pen in their hands had been like me.

It was almost a side-effect that this caused me to educate myself to a degree which was beyond anything a school could hope to achieve. My own appetite for knowledge and reading and connection had led me, and that is how education works, not by spoon-feeding, but by stimulating the appetite so that children cannot wait to feed themselves. Between the ages of twelve and fourteen I read hundreds and hundreds of books, but more importantly I became *unafraid* of reading. Great Writers, I discovered, were not to be bowed down before and worshipped, but embraced and befriended. Their names resounded through history not because they had massive brows and thought deep incomprehensible thoughts, but because they opened windows in the mind, they put their arms round you and showed you things you always knew but never dared to believe. Even if their names were terrifyingly foreign and intellectual-sounding, Dostoevsky, Baudelaire or Cavafy, they turned out to be charming and wonderful and quite unalarming after all. Late Henry James was a struggle, I will confess, and some of the longer sentences in Proust would lose me entirely, but all in all, by the time I was fourteen I knew that being gay was a kind of dark blessing, an awful privilege and I knew that, as Oscar once wrote on a photograph to an admirer, 'The secret of life is in art.'

Without libraries none of this would have been possible. They are still to me places of incredible glamour, possibility, power, excitement and pleasure. Of course the worldwide web and the wonders of the digital age, as well as advances in social understanding, decency and common sense make it less likely that a gay teenager need ever grow up feeling alone, but the downside to that huge advance is that that same teenager may never be led to those magical municipal labyrinths whose shelves contain so much and the existence of which for the better part of two hundred years has so immeasurably improved the quality of so many millions of ordinary lives.

THE SECRET LIFE OF LIBRARIES

BELLA BATHURST

You can tell a lot about people from the kinds of books they steal. Every year, the public library service brings out a new batch of statistics on their most pilfered novelists – Martina Cole, James Patterson, Jacqueline Wilson, J.K. Rowling. But in practice, different parts of Britain favour different books. Worksop likes antiques guides and hip-hop biographies. Brent prefers books on accountancy and nursing, or the driving theory test. Swansea gets through a lot of copies of the UK Citizenship Test. Liverpool prizes Arnold Schwarzenegger's thoughts on bodybuilding. In Barnsley, it's MIG welding and tattoos ('I've still no idea what MIG welding is,' says Ian Stringer, retired mobile librarian for the area. 'The books always got taken before I could find out.') And Marylebone Library in London has achieved a rare equality. Their most stolen items are the *Jewish Chronicle*, Arabic newspapers and the Bible.

But the figures show something else as well – that amongst all communities and in all parts of Britain, our old passion for self-improvement remains vivid. Unlike DVDs or CDs or Xbox games, books removed from public libraries have no resale value. Unless they're very rare or very specialist, even hardbacks aren't worth anything any more. So the only reason to take books is to read them.

Even so, theft remains a sensitive subject. 'If someone suggested the idea of public libraries now, they'd be considered insane,' says Peter Collins, Library Services Manager in Worksop. 'Because libraries are based on trust. I mean, if you said you were going to take a little bit of money from every taxpayer, buy a whole load of books and music and games, stick them on a shelf and tell everyone, 'These are yours to borrow and all you've got to do is bring them back,' they'd be laughed out of government.' But theft – or loss, or forgetting – is not a new thing. During the 1930s, supposedly a far more upright age, 8.8 million books vanished from the library system every year. Some areas made an industry of it. In Edinburgh during the '60s and '70s, handfuls of books used to be hurled out of the Central Library windows into waiting vans every time there was a fire alarm, and the railway staff at nearby Waverley station once rang the library to say they'd found a whole carriage-load of stolen stock.

In Worksop, Peter Collins radiates passion for his job, a love both of libraries and for the infinite variety of people who use them. He's thirty-three and 'always defined myself by being a librarian. I'd say to girls, 'Guess what I do for a living?!' Admittedly, they were the kind of girls who might be impressed by an MA in librarianship, but I was just so proud of it, so in love with what I did. When I first met my future wife, she got a tirade about the magic of libraries.'

Which doesn't quite conform to the old image of librarians as diffident, mole-eyed Philip Larkin types, or of disappointed spinsters with limited social skills who spent their time blacking out the racing pages and censoring Page 3. A list of books once considered morally suspect by librarians in the US includes *Catch-22*, *The Adventures of Huckleberry Finn*, *The Catcher in the Rye*, *Wuthering Heights*, *1984*, *Brave New World* and *Moby Dick*. 'In the '60s before the *Lady Chatterley* trial', says Ian Stringer, 'you used to get block books – literally, wooden blocks in place of any books the librarians thought were a bit risque, like *Last Exit to Brooklyn*. You had to bring the block to the counter and then they'd give you the book from under the desk. So of course you got a certain type of person just going round looking for the wooden blocks.'

Many libraries now recruit from the private sector – from retail, marketing or customer-service backgrounds. Librarians are still supposed to be people who love books but the new idea is that they quite like people too, and don't mind dealing with some of society's more 'challenging' individuals. Clearly, no genuine misanthrope would last for long in a profession which now spends much of its time helping adults with basic literacy skills, stopping drug use in the toilets, or providing creche facilities for toddlers.

There are 4,500 public libraries in Britain as well as almost a thousand national and academic libraries. As part of its programme of cuts, the coalition government wants to close around 500 public libraries around the country. Librarians – traditionally seen as a mild, herbivorous breed – are up in arms. Partly because public libraries are often seen as a soft target, partly because they say the government consistently undervalues the breadth of what they do, and partly because the cutting will be done during a recession, which is exactly when everyone starts going to the library again.

Some sense of the emotional value is given by the writer Mavis Cheek, who ran workshops within both Holloway and Earlstoke prisons. At Earlstoke, she had groups of eight men who 'may or may not have done unspeakable things', but who enjoyed the freedom of the writing groups so much they ended up breaking into the prison library when they found it shut one day, risking the withdrawal of their privileges in order to do so. Which authors did the prisoners like most? 'Graham Greene,' says Cheek.'All that adventure and penance. His stuff moves fast, it's written very sparely, and it's direct.'

Greene might seem a surprising choice, but then what people choose to read *in extremis* often is. Within the first six months of the Second World War, library issues across Britain had risen by 20 per cent, and in some areas by 50 per cent. Evacuees and women whose sons or husbands were away fighting – people, in other words, who had the strongest need to see the world otherwise – were amongst their keenest users. In London, some authorities established small libraries in air-raid shelters. The unused Tube station at Bethnal Green had a library of 4,000 volumes and a nightly clientele of 6,000 people. And what those wartime readers chose were not practical how-to manuals on sewing or home repairs, but philosophy. Plato and his *Republic* experienced a sudden surge in popularity, as did Schopenhauer, Bertrand Russell, Bunyan and Burton's *Anatomy of Melancholy*. Meanwhile on the battlefront itself, soldiers sought adventure. During the First World War a war library was established to supply over 1,800 hospitals at home and abroad with the works of Jack London, Rudyard Kipling, Conan Doyle, Rider Haggard and Robert Louis Stevenson.

Ian Stringer worked in Barnsley after the 1980s miners' strike. 'Barnsley hated Scargill. I mean, really *hated* him. Because he was their man, he was from Barnsley, they'd supported him, and he'd lost them the just cause. So all the mining jobs had gone and then all the auxiliary jobs like shops and engineering companies making machinery for the collieries had gone, and there was nothing for people any more, nothing at all. Library issues doubled during the strike, they were the highest they've ever been. A lot of ex-miners wanted books on law because they wanted to challenge the legality of what the government was doing. Or they needed practical self-help stuff like books on growing your own, or just pure escapism.'

As Kerry Pillai in Swansea points out, the same thing is happening now. 'When people lose their jobs, the first things many people do to save money is to get rid of the computers and the Sky TV contract. But if they're looking for a job, they need to be online. We've got sixty-five terminals here, our customers get two hours' free internet use each day, and we run CV workshops and sessions with the Job Centre. Libraries are a lifeline.' Or, as another senior librarian puts it, 'Nobody knows it, but we're the secret social service.'

The great unsold truth of libraries is that people need them not because they're about study and solitude, but because they're about connection. Connection with other worlds and different views, even if that's no more than being among other people thinking and breathing. Paul Forrest worked first in

Brent and now in Richmond – geographically close, but economically miles apart. He used to go out with the mobile library around the deprived areas of Edmonton. 'It was quite shocking how isolated people are sometimes.There's people out there who haven't left their homes in years. They need oxygen canisters to breathe, so they can only walk as far as the plastic lead allows them to. It's like a dog on a chain. Sometimes books or talking books are the only connection to the world they've got. And the mobile librarians really know their customers' interests – not just that they like romances, for instance, but romances with a bit of spice, not too much sex, a bit of history. Those books are almost a form of medication; I reckon we save the NHS a fortune in anti-depressants.' Not for long. If the rise in e-books continues, then in theory anyone with a computer would be able to 'borrow' the digitised text or audio version online. They wouldn't need the vans and the librarians; that last contact with humanity would vanish.

Because they provide a haven and because they don't discriminate about who they admit, libraries can often end up attracting problems. In some areas, their attempts to counteract drug use in the toilets has had mixed results. Some tried installing infra-red cameras, which should in theory prevent anyone trying to shoot up from being able to find a vein. The cameras worked great until someone realised that all users had to do was mark themselves up beforehand with a poster pen.

Libraries also have odder uses. Tramps and the homeless have always used libraries, since they're warm and full of comfortable spots in which to sleep. In Edinburgh, the Central Library is just up the hill from what used to be the city's main doss-house in the Grassmarket, so when the homeless were pushed back out onto the streets every morning, they'd head straight to the library for the day. Security apparently took a 'compassionate' view, as long as no one was being disruptive or smelt too much.

In Marylebone, they still take a lenient view. 'As long as they're vertical, it's alright,' says Nicky Smith, senior librarian. 'If they're horizontal or snoring, then we wake them up. Mind you', she adds cheerily, 'we were always told to wake people well before closing time, because if they turn out to be dead, then you won't get home before midnight.' Marylebone has particular cause to be vigilant; it has the unusual distinction of being one of the few libraries in Britain where someone *has* actually died. Edgar Lustgarten was well-known as a TV personality during the '50s and '60s. He presented an early version of *Crimewatch,* talking the viewers through the topical murder mysteries of the day. On the 15th of December 1978 he went to the library as usual and was found some time later dead at his desk. What had he been doing? 'Reading *The Spectator.*'

And of course every library has its stock of regulars. One Home Counties library had an old lady who walked around town with 'a massive proper talking pirate's parrot' on her shoulder. The parrot was chatty but conversationally limited, and since both it and its owner used the library's computers every day, the staff eventually had to put a notice up banning pets. Shortly after that, there was the unscheduled mobility-scooter ram-raid. 'There was an old lady who came in on her scooter, and I think she must have lost control and pressed the accelerator. I just remember us all standing there at the desk, watching her heading straight for the crime section. All the books and the shelves came down on top of her. It took ages to get her out – I don't think she knew how to get it into reverse.'

Issues and recommendations continue to present a challenge. Peter Collins: 'I regularly get people saying, "I took a book out of the library about ten years ago. It were blue. Have you still got it?" In Marylebone, one member of the House of Lords comes in every day to check the Peerage, presumably to find out if any undesirable types have tried sidling into the nobility overnight. 'One of our oddest requests came from the council,' says Ian Stringer in South Yorkshire. 'They asked us for an assessment of outcomes, not output. Output was how many books we'd stamped out, and outcome was something that had actually resulted from someone borrowing a book. So say someone took out a book on mending cars and then drove the car back, that's an outcome, or made a batch of scones from a recipe book they'd borrowed. It lasted until one of the librarians told the council they'd had someone in borrowing a book on suicide, but that they'd never brought it back. The council stopped asking after that.'

Odder still was Worksop's resident book-eater. 'We kept noticing that pages had been ripped from some of the books,' says Peter Collins, 'Not whole pages, just little bits. It would always be done really neatly, just the tops of the pages. And then we started noticing these little pellets everywhere, little balls of chewed paper cropping up in different parts of the library. Eventually, we figured out who it must be. None of us wanted to say we'd noticed him munching away at the books, so I approached him and said something like I'd noticed "tearing" on some volumes. He said he didn't know anything about it, but we've never seen him back. And we had a streaker once. In Tamworth. He got into the lifts, and somewhere between the first and the second floors he managed to take off all his clothes, run naked through Music and Junior, and then vanish out the front doors. The library there is right next to a graveyard, so goodness only knows what happened to him. All part of life's rich tapestry.'

It's an odd thing that libraries – by tradition temples to the unfleshly – can sometimes seem such sexy places. Perhaps it's their churchiness or the deep, soft silence produced by so many layers of print, or simply the hiding places provided by the shelves. 'There's a big following on the internet for sites on librarians and people with library fetishes,' says Kerry Pillai, manager at Swansea library. 'I don't know why. But we do have a lot of attractive staff here.' Has she ever been approached? 'I did get sniffed once,' she says. 'In the lifts.'

For many years, Ian Stringer worked on Barnsley's mobile libraries. So potent was the South Yorkshire service that at one point during the '80s, we had four couples leaving their spouses for each other. We ended up calling it the Mile Out Club.' What was going on? 'I think it's because you used to have two people going out, usually a man and a woman, in the van sometimes for nine hours at a stretch. Often it would be an older man and a younger woman, and I reckon some of the younger women had married young, and this was the first chance for them to see what an older man could be like. And some of the spots they'd get out to, like the farms, they'd be quite secluded. Not that anyone ever delayed the service, of course.' By the time the fourth couple got together, the erotic charge of the vans had grown so great that 'all the relatives ended up having a fight on the loading bay, everyone pitching in, all chucking boxes of library tickets at each other'.

Back in Worksop, Peter Collins is still keeping the faith. Books are not dead, reading still matters and the need for libraries is just as vital now as it was during the 1940s when Philip Larkin complained of stamping out so many books in a week he ended up with a handful of blisters. 'Reading is a much more alien concept for a lot of kids,' says Collins. 'The pace of life is different now, and people expect art to happen to them. Music and film do that, a CD will do that, but you have to make a book happen to you. It's between you and it. I always have a sense of trepidation when I open a book, because when you start reading you're giving yourself over to it, entering another person's world, opening yourself up. It's a relationship, and like any relationship, it can also make you feel guilty or resentful or happy or relieved. There's something of the importance and power of books that doesn't come from anything else. Nothing else has that magic, that combination of ink and discovery. Some people find books scary, but that's just an indication of their power. You're never going to get that mischievous sense of danger from a computer.

'People can be changed by books, and that's scary. When I was working in the school library, I'd sometimes put a book in a kid's hands and I'd feel excited for them, because I knew that it might be the book that changed their life. And once in a while, you'd see that happen, you'd see a kind of light come on behind their eyes. Even if that's something like 0.4 per cent of the population that ever happens to, it's got to be worth it, hasn't it?'

THE BOOKSTEPS

China Miéville

When she came to school the next day, Deeba's bag was packed. It contained sandwiches and chocolate and crisps and a drink, a penknife, a notepad and pens, a stopwatch, a blanket, plasters and bandages, a sewing kit, a wad of out-of-date foreign money she'd gathered from the backs of drawers all over her house, and other bits and pieces that she thought might just be useful. On top of them all Deeba had put her umbrella.

That morning she'd hugged each of her family members for a long time, to their amused surprise. 'I'll see you later,' she'd said to her brother Hass. 'I might be away for a while. But there's something I have to do.'

She reminded herself several times that her plan might not work. That all her preparations might

come to nothing. Still, her heart was going very fast most of the day. She thought it was excitement; then she thought it was fear. Then she realised it was both.

That morning she didn't talk to anyone. Becks

was watching her suspiciously and Zanna looked confused. Deeba ignored them.

At lunchtime she went to the school library.

There were a few other pupils in the room, doing homework, reading, working at the computers. Mr Purdey, the librarian, glanced up at her, then went back to his paperwork. Apart from a few whispers, the room was quiet.

Deeba walked past the desks and the other children and in among the bookshelves. She went to the furthest end of the room and stared at the shelves in front of her. She pulled on the glove made of paper and words.

The multicoloured spines of hardback novels stared back. They were slightly battered and coated in clear plastic. Deeba looked up. The shelves rose a metre or so above her, to the ceiling.

'Right,' whispered Deeba. She checked the contents of her bag one more time. 'Enter by booksteps,' she said, reading her hand. 'And storyladders.'

No one was watching. She stepped up carefully and put a foot on to the edge of a shelf, then reached up and took hold of another. Slowly, carefully she began to climb the bookshelves like a ladder. One foot above the other, one hand above the other.

The books didn't leave much space for her fingers or toes. She felt the bookshelves wobble, but they didn't collapse. Deeba concentrated on reading the titles just in front of her fingertips.

She knew she must be close to the ceiling. She

didn't slow and she didn't look up. She stared straight ahead at the books and climbed.

A little way up the spines looked less battered. Their colours more vivid. Their titles less familiar. Deeba tried to remember if she had ever heard of *The Wasp in the Wig*, or *A Courageous Egg*.

It took a moment for her to realise that she was still climbing. The library floor looked further down than it should be. In front of her was a book called *A London Guide for the Blazing Worlders*. Deeba kept climbing. She was definitely beyond where the ceiling had been. Still she didn't look anywhere but straight in front.

She clung to the edges of the shelves and climbed for a long time. A wind began to buffet her. Deeba tore her gaze from a book called *A Bowl for Shadows* and at last looked down. She gave a little scream of shock.

Far, far below her she saw the library. Children walked between the shelves like specks. The bookshelf she was ascending rose like a cliff edge, all the way down and as far to either side as she could see.

Vertigo made Deeba nauseous. She had to force herself to keep going up.

She stopped to rest when her arms and legs were shaking. By this time all she could see was an endless stretch of bookshelf. Behind her back was nothing but darkness.

Deeba tried to take a book off the shelf to take a look inside it. She almost lost her grip. She heard

86

herself shriek and she clung to the storyladder while her heart slowed.

She wondered if her friends below would hear a tiny tinny sound, and if she fell whether she would keep tumbling until she landed back in the library.

Eventually she fished her umbrella out of her bag and climbed like a mountaineer, hooking a shelf high above with its curved handle and hauling herself up.

Once there was a hard squawking and a noise from the void behind her. Something approached her on wings.

Without looking, Deeba grabbed a handful of books and flung them over her shoulder, rustling like rudimentary wings. There was a thud and an angry cawing. The avian noise receded. She did not hear the books land.

Though relieved, Deeba felt vaguely guilty about mistreating them.

She stopped being aware of time. She was conscious only of an endless succession of titles and of wind growing stronger and louder and of darkness around her. Deeba's fingers closed on leaves. She went through places where ivy had claimed the shelves and tangled roots into the books. She went through places where little animals scuttled out of her way.

I might be climbing the rest of my life, she thought, almost dreamily. I wonder how far this bookcliff goes. *I wonder if I should maybe start moving left. Or right. Or diagonally.*

It was growing slowly lighter. Deeba thought she heard a low noise of talking. With a sudden shock, she realised that there were no more shelves.

She had reached the top. She reached up and hauled herself over the top of the wall of books and looked out over UnLondon.

Deeba clung exhausted. Below and all around her was the abcity. The loon shone down. She was so tired and confused that for several moments she could not make much sense of what she saw. She hooked her umbrella carefully over bricks and swung her leg over. Then she looked around.

Deeba swayed giddily. The wind pushed her hard.

She was straddling the rim of an enormous tower. It was a cylinder, at least a hundred feet in diameter, hollow and book-lined. Outside, bricks went down the height of countless floors past small clouds and flocking bats to UnLondon's streets. Inside, it was ringed with the bookshelves she had climbed. The vertical tunnel of books was dim, but lights floated at irregular intervals in the dark void below. It didn't seem to end. It wasn't a tower: it was the tip of a shaft of books that went deep into the earth.

At some point during her ascent, what had been a flat shelf-cliff must have curled around and joined up behind her back, so gradually she hadn't detected it. It had become a chimney poking from a vertical universe of bookshelves.

There was motion below her. There were people on the shelves.

They clung to the edges of the cases and moved across them in expert scuttles. They wore ropes and hooks and carried picks on which they sometimes hung. Dangling from straps they carried notebooks, pens, magnifying glasses, ink pads and stamps.

The men and women took books from the shelves as they went, checked their details, leaning against their ropes, replaced them, pulled out little pads and made notes, sometimes carried a book with them to another place and reshelved it there.

'Hey!' Deeba heard. A woman was climbing towards her. Several men and women turned in their tethers and looked curiously.

'Can I help you?' the woman said. 'I think there's been some mistake. How did you get past reception? These shelves aren't open-access.'

'Sorry,' said Deeba. 'I don't know what you mean.'

The woman moved like a spider just below her. She looked at Deeba over the top of her glasses.

'You're supposed to put in a request at the front desk and one of us'll fetch whatever you're after,' she said. 'I'm going to have to ask you to go back.' She pointed over at UnLondon.

'That's where I want to go,' Deeba said, pulling off the glove and putting it in her bag. 'But I came from inside.'

'Wait . . . really?' the woman said excitedly. 'You're a traveller? You came by storyladder? My goodness. It's been years since we've had an explorer. It's not an easy journey after all. Still, you know what they say:

89

"All bookshelves lead to the Wordhoard Pit." And here you are.

'I'm Margarita Staples.' She bowed in her harness. 'Extreme librarian. Bookaneer.'

(This is an extract from China Miéville's novel *Un Lun Dun*, published by Macmillan.)

ALMA MATER

CAITLIN MORAN

Home-educated and, by seventeen, writing for a living, the only alma mater I have ever had is Warstones Library, Pinfold Grove, Wolverhampton.

It was a low, red-brick box on grass that verged on wasteland, and I would be there twice a day – rocking up with all the ardour of a clubber turning up to a rave. I read every book in there – not really, of course, but as good as; when I'd read all the funny books, I moved on to the sexy ones, then the dreamy ones, the mad ones, the ones that described distant mountains, idiots, plagues, experiments.

I sat at the big table and read all the papers; on a council estate in Wolverhampton, the broadsheets were as incongruous and illuminating as an Eames lamp.

The shelves were supposed to be loaded with

books – but they were, of course, really doors; each book-lid opened was as exciting as Alice putting her gold key in the door. I spent days running in and out of other worlds like a time bandit or a spy. I was as excited as I've ever been in my life in that library, scoring new books the minute they came in; ordering books I'd heard of, then waiting, fevered, for them to arrive, like they were Word Christmas.

I had to wait nearly a year for *Les Fleurs du Mal* by Charles Baudelaire to come; even so, I was still too young to think it anything but a bit wanky, and abandoned it twenty pages in for Jilly Cooper.

But *Les Fleurs du Mal*, man! In a building overlooked by a Kwik Save, where the fags and alcohol were kept in a locked metal cage lest they be stolen! Simply knowing that I could have it in my hand was a comfort in this place so very, very far from anything extraordinary or exultant.

Everything I am is based on this ugly building on its lonely lawn – lit up during winter darkness, open in the slashing rain – which allowed a girl so poor she didn't even own a purse to come in twice a day and experience actual magic: travelling through time, making contact with the dead (Dorothy Parker, Charlotte Brontë, Richard Brautigan, Truman Capote).

A library in the middle of a community is a cross between an emergency exit, a life raft and a festival. They are cathedrals of the mind; hospitals of the soul; theme parks of the imagination. On a cold, rainy island, they are the only sheltered public spaces where you are not a consumer, but a citizen instead. A human with a brain and a heart and a desire to be uplifted, rather than a customer with a credit card and an inchoate 'need' for 'stuff'.

A mall – the shops – are places where your money makes the wealthier wealthy. But a library is where the wealthy's taxes pay for you to become a little more extraordinary instead. A satisfying reversal. A balancing of the power.

After protests, injunctions have been granted to postpone library closures, followed by full judicial reviews of councils over their closure plans. As the cuts kick in, protesters and lawyers are fighting for individual libraries like dog-walkers pushing stranded whales back into the sea.

A public library is such a potent symbol of a town's values; each one closed down might as well be 6,000 stickers plastered over every available surface reading: 'WE CHOOSE TO BECOME MORE STUPID AND DULL'.

Although I have read a million words on the necessity for the cuts, I have not seen a single letter on what the exit plan is: what happens in four years' time, when the cuts will have succeeded, and the economy gets back to 'normal' again. Do we then – prosperous once more – go round and re-open all these centres, clinics and libraries, which have sat, dark and unused, for nearly half a decade?

It's hard to see how – it costs millions of pounds

to re-open deserted buildings, and cash-strapped councils will have looked at billions of square feet of prime real estate with a coldly realistic eye.

Unless the government has developed an exit strategy for the cuts, and has insisted that councils not sell closed properties, by the time we get back to 'normal' again, our Victorian and postwar and '60s red-brick boxy libraries will be coffee shops, Lidls and pubs. No new libraries will be built to replace them. These libraries will be lost forever.

And in their place, we will have a thousand more public spaces where you are simply the money in your pocket rather than the hunger in your heart. Kids – poor kids – will never know the fabulous, benign quirk of self-esteem of walking into 'their' library and thinking: 'I have read 60 per cent of the books in here. I am awesome.' Libraries that stayed open during the Blitz will be closed by budgets.

A trillion small doors closing.

THE LIBRARY OF BABYLON

TOM HOLLAND

In one of his most celebrated fictions, Jorge Luis Borges imagined an entire universe that was a library. Hexagons lined with books extend forever, 'one after another, endlessly'. Contained within the infinitude of these hexagons is every book that has ever existed. Before the chilling eternity of the library's vastness, it is not the books themselves but humanity that is menaced by ruin. 'I am perhaps misled by old age and fear', the anonymous narrator confesses, 'but I suspect that the human species – the *only* species – teeters at the verge of extinction, yet that the Library – enlightened, solitary, infinite, perfectly unmoving, armed with precious volumes, pointless, incorruptible, and secret – will endure.'

Even by the incomparable standards of Borges, the fantasy is a dazzling one. Role reversal is invariably unsettling. The truth is, of course, that the library has never existed that was not shadowed by an apprehension of its own mortality. Borges himself knew this better than anyone. His fiction is haunted by the vanished libraries, and the vanished books, of our own world, in which 'the gnostic gospel of Basilides' and 'the lost books of Tacitus' do not sit waiting to be discovered on the shelf of some hexagon, but instead have been destroyed forever. To look at a library is to know that its volumes can be burned, its shelves cleared and emptied, its walls left an empty shell. It is to feel – even in this age of digital abundance – a sense of the precariousness and the preciousness of human knowledge.

Borges titles his fiction 'The Library of Babel'. It alludes to the great city in the first book of the Bible, whose inhabitants sought to build a tower that would reach to the heavens, and were punished by God with a multiplicity of languages, so that they were left unable to 'understand one another's speech'. Yet although the Bible itself attributes the name of Babel to an echoing of the Hebrew verb '*balal*' – 'to confuse' or 'mix' – it also has another source. Babel is Babylon, and the great tower commemorated in the Bible is the vast ziggurat, formed out of seventeen million bricks and looming almost a hundred metres high, that once dominated the giant city. Time would see both 'become a heap of ruins, the haunt of jackals, a horror and a hissing, without inhabitant' – and yet the glamour and mystique of Babylon's name would long outlive its ruin. If the city was commemorated by Jews and Christians as the very archetype of worldly greatness brought low, then so also was it remembered by them as something rather different: the great repository of humankind's primordial wisdom.

A whole millenium after Babylon had lost her independence for good, and five hundred years after the birth of Christ, it was still recalled that the mudflats stretching between the two great rivers of the Tigris and the Euphrates – 'Mesopotamia', as it was known in Greek – had provided humanity with the original wellspring of its learning. By AD 500, libraries filled with the wisdom of Jewish and Christian scholars dotted the landscape, and the idols of Babylon had long since been toppled and destroyed. What had not vanished, though, was a sense of awe at the sheer antiquity and scale of the learning once commanded by the Babylonian priests. A story was told of how workmen digging amid the Mesopotamian mud had once stumbled across a whole buried library. The books, when they were deciphered, had been found to contain the wisdom of the generations who had lived before Noah's Flood. Clearly, then, a land where such treasures still existed, waiting to be excavated, richly merited its reputation as the land 'where the true art of divination first made its appearance'.

Modern archaeology has confirmed the gist, if not the details, of this legend. Mesopotamia was indeed, just as the ancients always held it to be, the birthplace of the library. The oldest known example of one, excavated at the site of Nippur, in what is now southern Iraq, was already centuries old when Babylon first rose to greatness. Dating from the middle of the third millennium BC, it contained gazetteers, lists of gods, collections of hymns, and works of literature. The scribes who maintained the collection seem even to have issued a catalogue. Yet if its survival serves to demonstrate just how primordial is the desire of humans to assemble and systematise the sources of their knowledge, then so also does it bear witness to something far bleaker. The texts contained within the library of Nippur consisted of inscriptions pricked originally on wet clay – and the resulting tablets only lasted into the present because, at some point in their history, they were baked rock hard. An unknown conqueror, laying Nippur to waste, must have torched the building in which the tablets were being stored – and by burning it to the ground, preserved its contents for good. Right from the very beginning, then, it seems, libraries have embodied a certain paradox: that conservation and ruin can be sides of the same coin.

The warlords of ancient Mesopotamia, who never wasted any opportunity to illumine their own names, and to ride their chariots over the rubble of others' ambitions, certainly understood this. Tiglath-Pileser I, the Assyrian king who at the end of the second millennium BC set his city on such an intimidating and impregnable footing that for almost five hundred years it would be the most feared power in the Near East, was also the first man known by name to have founded a library. The association between pitiless wars of conquest and bibliophilia was clearly an enduring one in Assyria: the library founded by its last great king, Ashurbanipal, was on a scale that dwarfed anything that had gone before it. Collections of clay tablets, no less than slaves or gold, were highly prized by the Assyrians, who had only to capture an enemy city to start carting off its libraries. To the book-loving Ashurbanipal, rare texts ranked as the very pickings of conquest. All of them were duly branded with his stamp. 'Palace of Ashurbanipal', they read, 'King of Assyria, King of the World'.

But his vaunt would prove an empty one. In 612 BC, fifteen years after the death of Ashurbanipal, the Assyrian capital of Nineveh was sacked. The great royal library was put to the torch, and its collection of clay tablets – boastful stamps of ownership and all – baked solid by licking flames. Back in 648, Ashurbanipal had captured Babylon, and looted some 2,000 tablets; now, with the destruction of Nineveh, the Babylonians had their revenge. Over the ruins of the Assyrian Empire, they raised a dominion of their own. In the best traditions of Mesopotamian imperialism, they sacked cities, deported entire peoples – and lovingly built up libraries. Scholars pored over vast collections, borrowed tablets, even stole them. Some busied themselves with deciphering ancient inscriptions, recycling archaic phrases, looking to the distant past to legitimise the needs and whims of their masters. Others traced the turning of the ages of the world, scrupulously recording lists of kings, and compiling detailed star charts. Throughout Mesopotamia, a great network of observatories had been established, enabling astrologers to trace the warnings of the heavens, and speedily to dispatch news of them back to the intelligence chiefs in Babylon. This information was all of it stored in libraries. The ability to read the future and to map the patterns cast on statecraft by the stars had always been a potent weapon of the Babylonian kings. The instincts that made Babylon the capital of libraries were much the same, in the final reckoning, as those that had brought her victory over the Assyrians. Knowledge was power – and power was barely worth having without knowledge.

Even after Babylon had fallen in her turn – first, in 539, to the Persians, and then again, in 331, to Alexander the Great – the primordial Mesopotamian notion that libraries were markers of class did not fade. In time, indeed, it came to affect the entire interpretation of what had been, for two long centuries, an ongoing series of wars between the Greeks and the Persians, and which had only finally been brought to an end when Alexander finished off the Persian Empire for good. According to Aulus Gellius, an engaging Roman miscellanist, libraries had been directly in the front line of this conflict. The Persian king, not content with burning Athens, had made off with her public library; one of Alexander's generals, a century and a half later, had then made a point of sending it back. Alexander himself, it was confidently claimed, had planned to build the largest library ever seen directly on the site of Nineveh. Seleucus, a notoriously high-aiming general who managed to elbow his way to the throne of Babylon after the death of Alexander, was reputed to have taken this strain of megalomania even further. A century or so after his death, he was remembered with mingled horror and admiration as a man who had sought 'to burn all the books in the world, because he wanted the calculation of time to begin with himself'.

Tall stories one and all. The truth was that the Greeks – whose cities were a fraction of the size of Babylon, whose societies boasted no distinct scribal class, and whose economies had always managed perfectly well without state bureaucracies – had no tradition of libraries. It was only with Alexander's conquest of the fabulously ancient and sophisticated cities of Mesopotamia that their eyes were opened to what they had been missing. To the tough and brutal men who had served with Alexander as his lieutenants, and who then, on their master's death, carved up his massive kingdom among themselves, the possession of a library was an obvious way to signal their self-promotion from the ranks of *condottieri* to kings. The fantasies bred by the ambitions of these warlords served to demonstrate just how effectively libraries could stand proxy for freshly minted empires. Just as every king, in the wake of Alexander, dreamed of ruling the entire world, so their libraries were designed to serve them as the focus of a truly olympian conceit: that every book ever written could be gathered in a single place.

The story told of Seleucus, that he had aimed at a universal bonfire of libraries, found its mirror image in the founding by another of Alexander's generals of what remains, to this day, the world's most celebrated library. Ptolemy, a battle-hardened veteran who combined the instincts of a street-fighter with the tastes of a *littérateur*, had grabbed for himself the only kingdom that could rival Mesopotamia for sheer wealth and antiquity: Egypt. Indeed, in one obvious way, the land of the Nile was even better suited to the manufacture of books than the mudflats that surrounded Babylon. The ready availability of papyrus, a reed which grows in the marshes of the Delta, and can be flattened out to make a highly durable writing material, had enabled pen-pushers to inspect, measure and prescribe the lives of the Egyptians for millenia. Now, with the arrival in Egypt of a foreign and upstart dynasty eager to make a splash, papyrus came into its own. Settling in Alexandria, the great city founded on the Mediterranean shoreline by Alexander himself, Ptolemy and his heirs set about transforming their parvenu capital into the most formidable cultural power-house on the face of the planet. A great temple, filled with gardens, porticos and lodgings, was built right in the heart of the city, and dedicated to the Muses: a 'Museum'. Here, a resident community of scholars were to enjoy a royally-sponsored life of the mind, complete with 'free meals, large salaries, tax-exemptions, beautiful surroundings, good lodgings, and plenty of slaves'. Most crucially of all, they were to be provided with that lifeblood of scholarship: an immense collection of books. The Library, at its height, would contain a quite staggering number of scrolls – upwards of a million, by some estimates. Nothing quite like it had ever been seen before.

Yet the fame of the Library of Alexandria exists in the context of a familiar paradox. Rather as it was the incineration of clay tablets in Mesopotamia that ensured their ultimate survival, so has the celebrity of Ptolemy's great foundation long depended for its fantastical character upon the fact that it no longer exists. Nothing sheds a more glamorous light upon the legendary scale of the Library's holdings than the mystery of their destruction. Many culprits have been suggested. One theory holds that Julius Caesar accidentally incinerated the Library while he and Cleopatra were under siege in Alexandria – but although he is certainly recorded as having burnt a great quantity of books, these appear to have been scrolls stored in a warehouse beside the docks, rather than the holdings of the Library itself. Another legend, even more popular, claims that the classical world's greatest monument to learning was sacrificed upon the altar of religious savagery and ignorance. Edward Gibbon, in his great history of the decline and fall of the Roman Empire, fingered 'the mischievous bigotry of the Christians who studied to destroy the monuments of idolatry'. A Christian bishop, writing in the thirteenth century, had in turn pinned the blame on the Muslims. The Arab conqueror of Alexandria, after he had enquired of the Caliph what should be done with the contents of the great library, is said to have ordered them to be burnt. 'If their content is in accordance with the book of Allah, we may do without them, for in that case the book of Allah more than suffices. If, on the other hand, they contain matter not in accordance with the book of Allah, there can be no need to preserve them.' Into the flames the books of the Library duly went – and for six months, it is said, they kept the public baths well stoked. Both stories, however, are implausible in the extreme. The anecdote told of the Caliph has all the verisimilitude of a fable from the Arabian Nights, while Gibbon, in laying the blame for the vandalism upon an archbishop 'whose hands were alternately polluted with gold, and with blood', allowed his love of a solemn sneer at Christianity to trump his customary close attention to the sources. The mystery, then, abides. All we can really know for certain is that the Library and its precious contents did indeed vanish long ago. To call this a mystery, though, is perhaps to over-dignify it. 'I sincerely regret the more valuable libraries which have been involved in the ruin of the Roman empire', wrote Gibbon; 'but when I seriously compute the lapse of ages, the waste of ignorance, and the calamities of war, our treasures, rather than our losses, are the object of my surprise.' Alexandria may have boasted the most famous library in the world; but she was not the only city to have lost a great collection. In AD 267, a band of Germanic freebooters called the Heruli sacked Athens, and destroyed a library that had been founded by the Emperor Hadrian, no less. A hundred years later, and a noted scholar could lament that the libraries of Rome were as empty 'as tombs'. Even in Constantinople, the city that endured as a capital of a Roman Empire for almost a millenium after the extinction of the Empire in the West, only fragments of the libraries that had once adorned the palaces of the emperor and the patriarch survived their decrepitude. Deep in the countryside beyond Constantinople, an Arab ambassador reported in the tenth century, there stood a temple where the ancient pagans were said to have worshipped the stars, piled so high with manuscripts that it would have taken a thousand camels to carry them away – and all the maunscripts were crumbling into dust.

The ruin of the great libraries of antiquity, almost total as it was, cannot help but make for sobering reflection. 'Like the generations of leaves, the lives of men,' mourned Homer in the *Iliad*. Ptolemy, in founding his great library, had been moved – in part, at least – by a dread that the same might be true of books. The scholars who staffed it believed themselves to be shoring up civilisation against the ever-present threat of ruin. Their agents confiscated manuscripts from unwary visitors; they cheated cities like Athens of their literary heirlooms; they scoured the book markets of the Mediterranean, sniffing out rare titles and definitive editions. Yet for all the immeasurable debt of gratitude we owe the librarians of Alexandria, it is as well to remember that the physical transmission of manuscripts from classical antiquity into the Middle Ages and the Renaissance owed nothing to libraries founded by any emperor or king. What has come down to us today derived instead from altogether more marginal institutions: the equivalent of run-down libraries, perhaps, in a financially-squeezed inner city borough. Pages stuffed into a vase; papyrus scraps buried beneath the crumbling of provincial walls; musty folios stored in a monastery's vaults: these are what survived the obliteration of the ancient world's imperial collections of books.

Borges, in his fable of the universal library, imagined some of the heresies to which its inhabitants were prone. Among these the most seductive was worship of a figure named the Book-Man. 'On some shelf in some hexagon, it was argued, there must exist a book that is the cipher and perfect compendium *of all other books*, and some librarian must have examined that book; this librarian is analogous to a god.' Even in the Library of Babel, however, this was ultimately recognised to be an illusion. The perfect librarian, like the perfect library, does not exist. Today, more than ever before, the dream of possessing the ultimate in libraries, a collection which incorporates and renders accessible the complete sum of human knowledge, enthuses the mighty, the technologically proficient, the super-rich. A dazzling dream, to be sure – but one that runs the risk, perhaps, of blinding us to the value of altogether less glamorous libraries. Not every collection of books can embody the ambitions of an Ashurbanipal, a Ptolemy, a Google. A civilisation must be judged as well by the books it keeps in institutions far removed from the centres of power.

Its very survival, after all, may ultimately depend upon it.

A CORNER OF ST JAMES'S

Susan Hill

It is always the Michaelmas term. It is always early dark with lights shining out of a thousand London windows. It is always cold and the air always smells of smoke. It is always foggy. I am always nineteen or twenty. I am always wearing my King's College royal blue and scarlet scarf. (Was mine the last generation to sport them? It was the first thing we bought on arriving, and in the Strand and down Surrey Street they knew when term had begun by the sighting of the first scarf, like the first swallow. Many things may be better there now, and I am not a sentimentalist about my university days, but it was a sad one when things went into reverse, and, instead of being an object of pride, the wide, warm, striped college scarf became one of ridicule.)

The old library in the Strand building at King's was

an excellent place but during term time the waiting list for essential books on the reading schedule was very long. They had three copies each of E.M.W. Tillyard's *The Elizabethan World Picture* and *The Complete Essays of Hazlitt* but there were thirty of us needing them both and even if I had had any money to buy books, there were precious few second-hand copies available to be bought – or not until the end of the year, when they were no longer needed.

Then one day, waiting to check a book in or out, I caught sight of a notice about the London Library, 14 St James's Square, SW – of which I had never heard. Below a brief description of the Library, I read about a scholarship offered to full-time undergraduates. Get a scholarship and membership was free for the three years of one's degree course.

It was October and dark early. It was foggy. It was cold. I wore my royal blue and scarlet scarf. And I walked into that historic Library for the very first time to pick up an application form, knowing, as I did so – I had read up about the Library – that I was walking in the footsteps of George Eliot and T.S. Eliot, Charles Darwin and Charles Dickens, Kipling and Carlyle, Virginia Woolf and Vita Sackville-West, Henry James and M.R. James . . . and, oh, everyone, everyone, heroes all, a roll call of great writers.

My application had to be sponsored by two existing London Library members and by my head of department at King's, Professor Geoffrey Bullough.

I took the form and headed to the Cromwell Road

and the home of two writers who had become my friends and patrons, C.P. Snow and his wife, Pamela Hansford Johnson. They signed my application form, Charles Snow wrote an accompanying letter of recommendation, and, a very short time later, I was walking back to 14 St James's Square again for the first time as a London Library student Member.

I have never been a country member of the Library. The joy of it was going there several times a week during term, collecting the books I needed to study, using the quiet corners in which to work – college libraries are not good for concentration, there is too much activity.

I think I learned as much from browsing in the book stacks of the London Library as I have done anywhere in my reading life. There is something extraordinarily liberating and exciting about being let loose in such a place, allowed to wander, pick out this and that, read a bit here, a page there, take out the book, then wander to another bay in search of something related to it. It is the self-education among books that few people, now, are privileged to have. Virginia Woolf describes the benefits of it in her *Diaries* and *Essays*, though in spite of being a member of the London Library later in life, her early book education took place in her father's library in their house in Hyde Park Gate, one of the great private libraries of that, or any other, day.

But it was not only books I encountered in those somewhat perilous stacks and I daresay that it is the same now; for every eminent writer worth the name is a member, and a contemporary student might bump into Tom Stoppard or Antonia Fraser or David Hare and be star-struck.

One of the latter-day writers of the Golden Age style of detective story was Nicholas Blake – the pseudonym of the then Poet Laureate C. Day-Lewis. It was easier for writers to go about unrecognised in those days, when television was in its infancy and the papers did not back up everything with a visual image, but Cecil Day-Lewis could rarely have gone incognito because he had the most memorable of faces, lined and wrinkled like a map, as well as a rather large head. So when he stood aside for me to pass him in the narrow LL bookstacks I was hyper-conscious of who he was.

Not, though, as conscious as I was of the small man with thinning hair and a melancholy moustache who dropped a book on my foot in the Elizabethan Poetry section some weeks later. There was a small flurry of exclamations and apology and demur as I bent down, painful foot notwithstanding, picked up the book and handed it back to the elderly gentleman – and found myself looking into the watery eyes of E.M. Forster. How to explain the impact of that moment? How to stand and smile and say nothing, when through my head ran the opening lines of *Howards End*, 'One may as well begin with Helen's letters', alongside vivid images from the Marabar Caves of *A Passage to India*? How to take in that here, in a small space among old volumes and a moment when time stood still, was a man who had been an intimate friend of Virginia Woolf? He wore a tweed jacket. He wore, I think, spectacles that had slipped down his nose. He seemed slightly stooping and wholly unmemorable and I have remembered everything about him for nearly fifty years.

I went back to the hostel and took out *Where Angels Fear to Tread*, read some pages, read the author biography, and had that sense of unreality that comes only a few times in one's life. The wonder of the encounter has never faded. Nor, indeed, has the wonder of bumping into T.S. Eliot on the front doorstep of a house in Highgate, though, strangely, I cannot now remember *whose* house, but there was a literary party to which I had been invited by some kind patron of young writers. So there I stood, while Eliot rang the bell and gave me a rather owlish but kindly smile as we waited. Once the door was opened to us he was absorbed into the throng and I saw him no more – but I can certainly still hear the voice of someone saying, on seeing him, 'Oh good, here's Possum!'

IT TAKES A LIBRARY . . .

MICHAEL BROOKS

When you are researching a book these days, it's tempting to rely on the internet. It's certainly invaluable: a huge swathe of research literature is there at all our fingertips. But that's when you know what you're looking for. Every book I find via an internet search has something to say that I already know about. In a library, on the other hand, that book is only a starting point. That book is surrounded by books on a similar subject – books that I didn't know about. You pick them up, flick through them, and find treasures – and wisdom – you would never otherwise have found.

Researching *Free Radicals* involved many trips to a university library that I regularly use. Those trips invariably resulted in a lot of 'wasted' time looking up and down the surrounding shelves, pulling out related books that looked interesting, and skimming through them.

There is so much in libraries that deserves an airing. There is little that can compare with the joy and value of discovering a book that you could only have come across by being in the same physical space. One example is *Possible Worlds*, a book J.B.S Haldane wrote in 1927.

Though I read it, *Possible Worlds* didn't make it into *Free Radicals*. But Haldane did make it in there because he is famous for having experimented on himself for wartime science (self-experiment is one of the 'anarchies' of science that shed so much light on what really motivates scientists). Haldane and his father investigated the effects of exposure to chlorine and mustard gas. J.B.S pioneered the science of scuba diving and decompression sickness, his experiments inducing crushed vertebrae, panic attacks and perforated eardrums (through which he could blow smoke). He was truly courageous, and his science made a difference in wartime events. British commandos applied Haldane's research to their diving routines, and the knowledge allowed them to defend and hold the crucial stronghold of Gibraltar when Hitler tried to take it.

Haldane was not alone in self-experimenting. 'A good many biologists experiment on themselves,' he wrote in *Possible Worlds*. Dying while trying to work out the mechanism behind communicable diseases is 'the ideal way of dying', Haldane says.

It's so admirable because scientists know that they are working with incomplete knowledge. 'I have no doubt that the theories to which I entrusted my life were more or less incorrect,' he says. Nonetheless, the working hypotheses were good enough to enable him to make reliable risk assessments.

My favourite chapter in the book is entitled 'The Duty of Doubt'. It is an overview of the value of taking a sceptical stance on everything – science included: 'science has owed its wonderful progress very largely to the habit of doubting all theories', Haldane points out. Haldane strides across some great moments of science in which doubt played a central role, then expands his theme to encompass religion and politics.

When a politician calmly goes back on a policy, 'his enemies accuse him of broken pledges; his friends describe him as an inspired opportunist', Haldane says. It is only a pre-scientific thought process in the electorate that create this dilemma for politicians, Haldane argues: if we were to allow politicians to use the scientific method, a politician could say, 'I am inclined to think the tariff on imported glass should be raised. I am not sure this is a sound policy; however, I am going to try it. After two years, if I do not find its results satisfactory, I shall certainly press for its reduction or even removal.'

Imagine that! Perhaps this should be filed under *Impossible Worlds*. But in the current political climate, food for thought, nonetheless. And this from the era when Laurel and Hardy were just becoming popular, and the first Model A Fords were gracing the showrooms. Far be it from me to discourage people from reading new books, but I can't help thinking there's still an awful lot we can learn from the old ones.

THE MAGIC THRESHOLD

BALI RAI

I've always considered libraries to be magical and warm places, full of excitement and wonder. I remember being six years old, and walking into St Barnabas library in Leicester, staring in awe at the rows of shelves and the thousands of books. I don't recall the first book I ever borrowed, but I do know that once I'd crossed what Barack Obama has rightly called a 'magic threshold', I was hooked. And I do mean hooked.

My father instigated my first visit. As the immigrant son of a Punjabi farmer, his exposure to books and education was sorely restricted. On moving to the UK, he found his life a struggle, working long hours at manual jobs that paid only basic wages. He wanted his children to better themselves, and my sister and I benefited from that desire. Even after my father fell ill, and could no longer take me himself, my love of libraries remained. In fact, it grew stronger, and it is the library and books that have made me the writer, and the person, that I am today.

Reading became a joy, particularly after I first encountered Roald Dahl. I had read great stories before discovering *James and the Giant Peach* – wonderful picture books and comics too – but that first Roald Dahl book sent my head into a spin. I remember marvelling at the world he'd re-imagined, and laughing at the slightly silly adult characters. I even argued with my friends at school about which fruits would make the best homes. The first 'story' I ever wrote was a word-for-word copy of small parts of the book, but with my name substituted for 'James'. It drew a smile and a shake of the head from my teacher, who told me to write my own ideas instead. I was seven years old and I started to dream.

Roald Dahl was like God or a magician back then. He never seemed like a real, everyday person that I might meet in the street. I never imagined that I'd ever be like him, able to make a living from writing stories. I thought that writers had to be old and posh and white. Or dead and posh and white. Most times I read a book, the characters were white too. Actually becoming a writer, seeing as I was the British-born son of Indian parents, seemed as remote as becoming an astronaut.

So I continued to visit the library, to read and to dream. I read every fiction book I could find, and joined the protagonists in their adventures across the world. I learned new words and ideas and my imagination went into overdrive. I started to pick up non-fiction and newspapers too, encouraged by the librarians, and developed a life-long love for facts and world affairs. The more I read, the better I did at school, and the more sense every lesson began to make. I even began to challenge the things I was being taught, much to the amusement of my teachers. At home, I found myself interpreting the news for my increasingly sick father, and filling out the forms my mother couldn't read or understand. By the time I turned eleven, I was reading well above my age.

That was when I discovered Sue Townsend. I say discovered but it was more like she exploded onto the scene. Her first book, *The Secret Diary of Adrian Mole*, was a revelation for me. Here was this ordinary, everyday woman, who lived in my home city and had written a best-selling story about the sort of pupil I could have been sitting next to in class. Every character was real, every street, every house. I didn't realise it until a few years later, but I had found my role model.

Suddenly I was writing furiously about the world I saw around me. I had already grown out of children's books, and the young adult novels I found in my school library weren't anywhere near challenging enough. One or two books made me sit up – S.E Hinton's *The Outsiders*, Douglas Adams' brilliant *Hitchhiker's Guide* series, and Bernard

Ashley's *The Trouble with Donovan Croft* come to mind – but on the whole I was uninterested, and not through any fault of the librarian. Realistic and challenging young adult novels that dealt with everyday issues seemed few and far between. Once again, it was public libraries that came to my aid. I began to borrow books from the adult section, from the classics to Stephen King and beyond. At first the library staff were suspicious of my borrowing, worried that I might be reading unsuitable material. Once I'd started talking to them about the books I'd read, however, they started recommending others. No genre remained off-limits, bar romance perhaps, and more importantly I began to read more challenging non-fiction too. Politics, science, anthropology, art: they named it, so I wanted to read about it.

Libraries have assisted each part of my development as a person, from childhood, through my teens and beyond university into adulthood. Too many of my peers from working-class families, with poorly educated parents, show that there's a direct correlation between success and reading for pleasure. Maybe I was lucky. Perhaps I was pushed in the right direction. Whatever the reasons, I would not be the person I am today if it wasn't for libraries.

Now I've become the writer I dreamt of being, and today libraries are just as important to me as they've always been. No amount of internet research or fancy website design can replace the simple and effective value of a well-stocked reference library or archive. No e-reader will ever replace the beauty of a fully formed, 3-D book. Technology has its place, but it would not even exist without books and libraries. I love the feel and smell of libraries. That magic, that power with which they entranced me as a child, will never fade. To steal Barack Obama's line again, the first time I stepped across that 'magic threshold', my life changed forever. For that I will always be truly grateful.

LIBRARIES ROCK!

Ann Cleeves

When I was growing up, the only books we owned were a fat and disintegrating copy of the complete works of Shakespeare and an equally ancient *Palgrave's Golden Treasury*. We didn't live near a town with a bookshop and it was way before Amazon. Besides, it would never have occurred to my parents to spend money on books. Still, we were a family of readers, a library family. We talked about books. The Saturday morning visit to the library was a ritual, as much a part of our lives as Sunday morning church. The librarian was Mrs Macgregor. All those years ago and I still remember her name, although those of my teachers are long forgotten. Mrs Macgregor turned me into a crime writer. She introduced me to Enid Blyton, and then to Malcolm Saville, mysteries with chases and pace and surprise endings. She remembered which titles I'd read and saved copies of those I hadn't under the counter, producing them, like a magician's rabbit from a hat as I walked through the door. So a visit to the library was a treat and an excitement, an almost theatrical experience. It provided colour and wonder in the drab post-war years of the '50s and early '60s.

And that's what we need from our libraries now: excitement and passion and the thrill of finding an author new to us. Those people who grew up with shelves of their own books missed out on the pleasure of communal reading, of discussing and sharing, of discovery in a public space. They see libraries as dull and rather worthy places. Worth keeping, of course, but not really for *them*, not for the people who get sent proof copies or who can afford to check the internet and buy the books they've seen reviewed in the broadsheets. (I'd love to know how many politicians, council members and professional writers, those who talk about libraries and make policies about them, actually belong to their local branch . . .)

I have a vested interest of course. Without the support of libraries I wouldn't be published today. There would be no *Vera* on the television, no Shetland Quartet. If libraries hadn't bought my early novels I'd have been dumped by my publisher long ago – nobody else much was buying them! Libraries can take a chance on new authors and support mid-listers, they can buy in short fiction and books in translation. Rather than the grey and dreary institutions of public perception, these should be places of innovation and experiment, where readers can take a chance on a book, pick one because they like the look of the cover or the title or because they see it returned by the gorgeous young man who lives in their street. After all, they have absolutely nothing to lose. The book will be free.

They should also be places of debate and disagreement. Most libraries now host reading groups. They are safe and democratic spaces for people to come together. A reader in a group in North Tyneside once said to me: 'Eh, pet, I'm greedy for reading.' She had no formal education, but she came alive in the sessions, taking a delight in disagreeing with the majority view, in championing a book which everyone else dismissed as trash. Supported by library authorities, I've set up reading groups in prisons, in rural pubs, in the Alaskan bush and at very literary literature festivals. In all these settings I've been recommended titles I would never choose for myself but which have, in a small way, changed my life.

The libraries I love best are the ones that encourage readers to take this sort of chance. I worked for a while in Huddersfield Library and there staff regularly pulled books from their normal alphabetical order – the Dewey Decimal System still remains a complete mystery to me though I worked there for five years – and set up what they called the Serendipity Collection. This was a place to browse, to come upon a book to suit my mood, to fall for a new author. In the Serendipity Collection I chanced on my first example of contemporary translated crime fiction, *The Depths of the Forest* by Eugenio Fuentes. I loved it and I've been hooked on Euro-crime ever since.

Some say that the internet has taken the place of the library. We can browse the web, read bookish blogs, tweet bookish tweets. But we can't pick up the book. We can't take it away and read it for free. And there's something sadly solitary and second-hand about the electronic experience of choosing books. It needed Mrs Macgregor, with her grey hair and her magician's smile and her vicarious enjoyment of my reading adventures, to capture my imagination and set me on my way.

But perhaps today's young people are too sophisticated to be captivated in the same way by books? Perhaps reading is too passive for them and there are other, more exciting interests to capture *their* imaginations? I don't think that's true at all. Back in Huddersfield we ran a thriving family reading group, where parents and carers and their children carved time out of their busy lives to share their enthusiasms. And reading isn't in competition with the other arts; it's essential to their understanding. Stories and ideas spark all forms of creativity and still books hold most of our stories and ideas.

One Sunday, Huddersfield Central Library opened its doors just for teenagers. We called the project 'Teenage Kicks'. We weren't sure how many young people would turn up but the response was astonishing. We attracted boys and girls of all kinds: moody, angst-ridden adolescents, the shy, the exhibitionist and the rebellious. That day they met writers, explored books through music and drama and painting. At the end of the day we invited comments. One girl wrote: *Libraries rock!*

Of course they do, but they will only rock if there's money to buy new books, to provide training so staff will have the confidence to interact with readers, to employ passionate, newly qualified librarians. Without money, libraries become sad and tired. Without an adequate book fund, the new authors get left out, so does the quirky, the innovative, the difficult. And if libraries don't support these writers, publishers won't commission them. Without money, libraries are tempted to buy what is certain to issue – and that's the material that you can find in every supermarket, the bestsellers, the easily promoted. Libraries aren't supermarkets; they're places of cultural importance, where magic happens and where dreams begin. Or at least they should be.

THE FIVE-MINUTE RULE

Julie Myerson

I wrote my first novel when I was thirteen. It was about some lions who escaped from Africa to settle in Kensington (a place I had never been to but liked the sound of). It filled two slim exercise books and was (I thought) rather brilliant. I sent it off to Jonathan Cape, asking if they could publish it in time for Christmas, so my friends could buy it. They said they couldn't publish it at all, but that they hoped to hear from me later in my career. My career! I was in heaven.

I began a new novel *Samantha* (well, hadn't Daphne du Maurier done okay with *Rebecca*?) and sent the first few extremely derivative chapters off to the woman herself. She was generous (or foolish) enough to write back – igniting a brief and touching correspondence that only fed my crazed self-belief. Meanwhile after school, I'd rush over to the County Library on Angel Row where, tucked away in an upstairs cubicle – I still remember the smell of unwashed men's trousers because it was also where the tramps came in to get warm – I'd spend hours pouring over *The Writers' and Artists' Yearbook*. That book, with its lists of agents and publishers, a practical, informed link to a world I could only dream of belonging to, was a source of intense and reliable inspiration to me.

I continued to dream, but real life (university, first job, love, babies) intervened, and at twenty-nine there I suddenly was with a home, a partner, one child born and another on the way. Panic set in. I had all of this and I still hadn't written a novel.

I was on maternity leave when, encouraged by my partner – who knew me well enough to know I would never be happy until I had at least completed one book – I sat down at an old Amstrad in our spare room. I had nothing in my head except a vague, disturbing image of a pregnant woman who had seen a ghost. I also had an aching back, a baby who cried to be fed, and a friend's advice ringing in my ears: tell yourself you're going to set aside five minutes a day. If you can't do more, don't worry. But never let a day go by without doing your five minutes.

It was good advice. Eighteen months – and another baby – later, I had written *Sleepwalking*. I had no idea whether it was publishable or not, but I knew

I'd taken the first step towards being a writer: I'd actually written something. I went straight back to *The Writers' and Artists' Yearbook* and sent it out to four agents. One was on holiday, one never replied, two immediately wanted to take me on. A month later, I had publishers in several countries and a substantial two-book contract which meant I could give up the day job. I still look back on that time and feel dizzy.

But when unpublished writers come now and ask me for advice, I find it hard to know what to say. Because in their quiet, heartfelt determination all I really see is myself. Every published writer has their own story, their own superstitions, rituals and systems, their individual, moments of serendipity. Every published writer remembers, with a little snag of worry, exactly how it felt not to be published, not even to know if you ever would be. So all I can tell you is what worked for me:

The five-minute rule is a good one. Of course you almost always end up writing for longer, but – especially for those with family and work commitments – it is gloriously undaunting. It somehow helps you scale that initial terrifying cliff-face of 'where will I ever find the time?'

When you're writing your first novel, don't torment yourself by reading Updike, Murdoch, Rushdie. Read only first novels. When they're brilliant, then it's liberating, exciting, inspiring. And when they aren't, well, believe me, it's also pretty inspiring. If this is publishable, then so is mine . . .

Hold on to your self-belief. Convincing yourself is half the battle. I decided to be a writer when, aged nine, I noticed that Shakespeare's work was really a little bit like mine. When, at thirteen, I wrote off to Daphne du Maurier, it was less for advice, more to trumpet myself as a fellow author. And if someone had told me all those years ago as I sat among the unwashed men and fantasised, that one day I'd be a proper enough author to be asked to write introductions to other people's books? Yes, I would have gasped in astonishment. But another secret part of me would have thought: But of course!

Lastly, and maybe most importantly, no excuses, don't put it off. There is no right moment, no perfect computer, no point whatsoever in waiting for a sabbatical, or for your kids to grow up, or even (big myth) for inspiration to strike. Ideas don't come from somewhere mysterious and magical. They come from a blank page or screen, a willingness to sit alone for hours and spend time in your own head, a desire to make something where there was once nothing. In other words, it's amazing how often people seem to forget the final, most obvious rule: the only way to be a writer is to write. Start now. Good luck!

P.S. And Cape did hear from me later in my career. I'm pleased to say they now publish my fiction.

IF YOU TOLERATE THIS ...

NICKY WIRE

It's hard not to feel utterly despondent at the current plight of public libraries. Along with the NHS and the BBC, our libraries are some of the few truly remarkable British institutions left. So often absolutely ordinary in appearance, a good library should offer escape routes down the most extraordinary avenues, pathways into different worlds from the one you've left outside. Ridding our villages, towns and cities of libraries, which are essential in shaping a nation's consciousness, seems like a direct attack on the soul of the country.

Libraries have always reassuringly been there when I've needed them. Blackwood Library in Wales helped me through my O- and A-levels. They have given my parents decades of pleasure, satiating their desire to read and learn. This country's greatest ever poet and one of the biggest influences on my life and work, Philip Larkin, was – of course – a librarian. My wife Rachel worked as a librarian across all the branches in Newport. My brother Patrick worked in Blackwood Library. I remember clearly my mother bringing home a biography of *Under the Volcano* author Malcolm Lowry during my teenage years. Here was a life that was truly beyond eccentricity, incredibly sad and fucked up. I was wholly drawn to the nihilistic, hyper-intelligent nature of Lowry's story. That was the turning point that made books so precious to me, part of the transformative process that would eventually make me almost fetishise books themselves. For these and countless other reasons, the public library was a key factor in shaping who I am today.

There's a tendency to resort to romantic cliche when talking about libraries; clearly in a digital age they aren't a 'sexy' alternative. Maybe I'm old-fashioned but I still believe that the core of libraries will always be printed words rather than screens or keyboards. In any town or city, you can walk in and pick up the works of T.S. Eliot or Bret Easton Ellis, extremes of taste that you can dip into and thumb through without having anyone nudging you to make a purchase. There really aren't many things in life that can enrich you for free yet ask for nothing in return.

As an utterly self-made band, in our formative stages we vociferously consumed high and low culture – magazines, literature and TV. Without money, libraries became something of a lifeline, offering a clear window on to a wider world. In the summer of 2009, the band were honoured to be asked to open the new Cardiff Central Library. For us, it seemed like a chance to give something back to Wales. Seeing one of our lyrics – 'Libraries gave us power', from 'A Design for Life' – inscribed on the opening plaque was in its own way as affecting as playing the Millennium Stadium.

That opening line was adapted from an engraving above the entrance to Pill Library in Newport that read 'Knowledge is power'. The weight of those almost Orwellian words became intertwined with an idea about what the miners had given back to society when they built municipal halls and centres across the country – beautiful-looking institutes that they proudly left for future generations. The lyric was me railing against what I saw as a flippancy pervading the country with the rise of Britpop, a wholesale adoption – and bastardisation – of working-class culture.

The double life of that song's opening line is one of the most amazingly serendipitous things that's happened during the life of the band. I still feel intensely proud when I hear it cited out of the context of the song, like recently when Lauren Laverne dropped it into a brilliant piece of polemic on *10 O'Clock Live*.

At the moment, it really does appear that the

establishment is back in control of Britain. After thirty years of semi-pluralistic governance, the establishment is pushing hard its own agenda. When you look at the cabinet, the millionaire's row in the front benches of Parliament looks like a very public-school coup. One of the most amazing things about public libraries remains their utter classlessness. You don't have to have gone to Eton to make the most out of a library. They aren't inhabited by the kind of people currently damning them. The closure of libraries in conjunction with tuition fees and the radical reorganisation of the NHS are symbolic of the blatant power grab of this fiasco of a government. There is a way of solving these problems – it's called higher taxation of the wealthiest 10 per cent of the country. In the '90s, I'd have gladly included myself in that bracket.

We need to cherish these things while they still exist. Seek solace, seek knowledge. Seek power.

(Nicky Wire was interviewed by Robin Turner.)

LIBRARY LIFE

ZADIE SMITH

Sometimes people ask me if I am from a bookish family. I find it a difficult question to answer. One answer would be no, not in the traditional sense. My father left school at thirteen and my mother at sixteen. But another answer is: Christ, yes, they really were. Like a lot of working-class English people, in the '50s and '60s my father found his cultural life transformed by Allen Lane's Penguin paperback revolution. Now anyone could read Camus or D.H. Lawrence or Maupassant, for no more than the price of a pack of fags. So he bought these books and read them, and then spent the rest of his life boasting about all those books he'd read back in the '50s and '60s. I think he read to prove that his class had not succeeded in wholly defining him, and when he'd proved that, he stopped reading. My mother is a different story. When my father met my mother, his mildly aspirational reading met with the force of her determined autodidacticism. Pretty much the only place my parents' marriage could be considered a match made in heaven was on their bookshelves.

I grew up in a council estate off Willesden Lane, a small flat decorated with books. Hundreds of them on my father's makeshift shelves, procured almost entirely by my mother. I never stopped to wonder where she got them from, given the tightness of money generally – I just read them. A decade later we moved to a maisonette on Brondesbury Park and my mother filled the extra space with yet more books. Books everywhere, arranged in a certain pattern. Second-hand Penguin paperbacks together: green for crime, orange for posh, blue for difficult. Women's Press books together, Virago books together. Then several shelves of Open University books on social work, psychotherapy, feminist theory. Busy with my own studies, and oblivious in the way children are, I didn't notice that the three younger Smiths were not the only students in that flat. By the time I did, my mother had a degree. We were reading because our parents and teachers told us to. My mother was reading for her life. About two-thirds of those books had a printed stamp on the inside cover, explaining their provenance: PROPERTY OF WILLESDEN LIBRARY. I hope I am not incriminating my family by saying that during the mid-'80s it seemed as if the Smiths were trying to covertly move the entire contents of Willesden Green Library into their living room. We were chronic library users. I can remember playing a dull game with my brother called 'Libraries', in which we forced a crowd of soft toys to take out books from the 'library' that was our bedroom. Ben pretended to stamp them (they were of course already stamped) while I lectured some poor panda about late fees. In real life, when it came to fees, I was the worst offender. It was a happy day in our household when my mother spotted a sign pinned to a tree in the high road: WILLESDEN GREEN BOOK AMNESTY. The next day we filled two black bin-bags with books and dragged them down the road. Just in time: I was about to start my GCSEs.

I've spent a lot of time in libraries since then, but I remember the spring of 1990 as the most intense study period of my life, probably because it was the first. To go somewhere to study, because you have chosen to, with no adult looking over your shoulder and only other students for support and company – this was a new experience for me. I think it was a new experience for a lot of the kids in there. Until that now-or-never spring we had come to the library primarily for the café or the cinema, or to meet various love prospects of whom our immigrant parents would not approve, under the cover of that all-purpose, immigrant-parent-silencing sentence: I'M GOING TO THE LIBRARY. When the exams came, we stopped goofing off. There's no point in goofing off in a library: you're acutely aware that the only person's time you're wasting is your own. We sat next to each other at the long white tables and used the library computers and did not speak. Now we were reading for our lives. After my exams I felt I owed those students a collective debt – all those John Kelly girls and John Kelly boys, kids from Hampstead Comp, and Aylestone (as it was known then) from La Swap and William Ellis. We may not have spoken to each other, except to ask for sharpeners or paper, but by turning up we acted as each other's conscience. A reason to stay another hour, and another hour after that. It was a community of individuals, working to individual goals, in a public space. It's short-sighted to think all our goals were bookish ones. I happened to be in the library in the hope it would lead me to other libraries, but my fellow students were seeking all kinds of futures: in dentistry, in social work, in education, in catering, in engineering, in management. We all learned a lot of things in Willesden Green Library, and we learned *how* to learn things, which is more important. I learned that 'Milton was of the devil's party without knowing it' and that the Brontës had a brother. I found out who Henry V was and what Malcolm X did. I came to understand why silence is necessary for serious study, and what the point of coffee is. I discovered that there exist people who write not just books, but books about books, and finding that out changed my life.

Still, it's important not to overly romanticise these things. Willesden Green Library was not to be confused with the British Library. Sometimes whole shelves of books would be missing, lost, depressingly defaced or torn. Sometimes people would come in just to have a conversation, while I bit my biros to pieces in frustration. Later I learned what a monumental and sacred thing a library can be. I have spent my adult life in libraries that make a local library like Willesden Green's, like Kensal Rise's, like Kilburn's, look very small indeed; to some people, clearly, quite small enough to be rid of, without much regret.

But I know I never would have seen a single university library if I had not grown up living a hundred yards from that library in Willesden Green. Local libraries are gateways – not only to other libraries, but to other lives. Of course I can see that if you went to Eton or Harrow or Winchester or Westminster – like so many of the present Cabinet – you might not understand the point of such lowly gateways, or be able to conceive why anyone would crawl on their hands and knees for the privilege of entering one. It has always been, and always will be, very difficult to explain to people with money what it means not to have money. If education matters to you, they ask, and if libraries matter to you, well, why wouldn't you be willing to pay for them if you value them? They are the kind of people who believe value can only be measured in money, at the extreme end of which logic lies the dangerous idea that people who do not generate a lot of money for their families cannot possibly value their families as people with money do.

My own family put a very high value on education, on bookishness, but it happened that they did not have the money to demonstrate this fact in a manner that the present government seems able to comprehend. Like many people without a lot of money, we relied on our public services. Not as a frippery, not as a pointless addition, not as an excuse for personal stagnation, but as a necessary gateway to better opportunities. Like millions of British people, we paid our taxes in the hope that they would be used to establish shared institutions from which all might benefit equally. We understood very well that there are people who have no need of these services, who really cannot see the point of them. Who have made their own private arrangements, in health-care and education and property and travel and lifestyle, and who have a private library in their own private houses. These days I also have a private library in my own private house. And I have a library in the university in which I teach. But if you've benefited from the use of shared institutions, you know that to abandon them once they are no longer a personal necessity is like Wile E. Coyote laying down a rope bridge between two precipices, only to blow it up once he's reached the other side – so that no one might follow him. Apart from anything else, you may not be as wily as you think you are. One day, you might find that back on the other side of that chasm is where you want to be. You might discover how quickly an afternoon with a toddler passes in a local library, quicker than practically anywhere else. You might urgently want to know something about your street in 1894. You might realise that giving

up smoking or writing a novel is easier to do when
you're one of a group of people all seated on some
fold-up chairs in a circle. It might strike you that
what you really want in life is silence. Despite the
many wonders of the internet, you might suddenly
long for the smell of old books.

But even if none of these things apply to you,
even if community is your idea of hell, the principle
remains. Community exists in Britain, and no matter
how many individuals opt out of it, the commons of
British life will always be the greater force, practically
and morally. Community is a partnership between
government and the people, and it is depressing to
hear the language of community – the so-called 'Big
Society' – being used to disguise the low motives of
one side of that partnership as it attempts to worm
out of the deal. What could be better, they suggest,
than handing people back the power so they might
build their own schools, their own libraries? Better
to leave people to the already onerous tasks of
building their lives and paying their taxes. Leave the
building of infrastructure to government, and the
protection of public services to government – that
being government's mandate, and the only possible
justification for its power. That the grotesque losses
of the private sector are to be nationalised, cut from
our schools and our libraries, our social services
and our health service – in short, from our national
heritage – represents a policy so shameful I doubt
this government will ever live it down. Perhaps it's

because they know what the history books will make of them that our politicians are so cavalier with our libraries: from their point of view, the fewer places where you can find a history book these days, the better.

THE LENDING LIBRARY

KATE MOSSE

I first saw her on a Thursday afternoon. She was ahead of me on the path, walking fast as if to keep an appointment. Her hands were dug deep in her pockets and her shoulders hunched. A green belted jacket and pleated skirt, white shirt just showing above the collar and shoes suitable for pavements, not mud. Seamed stockings. Later, I realised why she looked familiar and why the look of her struck a false note. But not then. Not that first time.

I stopped, puzzled I'd not noticed her before. The path, at this point, was narrow and accessed only from Mill Lane, and though I usually walked down to the estuary in the afternoon, when I could get away, it wasn't a popular destination. Although the lights of the Lending Library were visible on the far side of the field, most local people avoided the path.

Too deserted, a bit too wild and overgrown and that November it had rained and rained.

She was too far ahead to make out her features and, besides, she didn't turn round. But her brown hair, visible beneath the rim of her cap, looked salon curled and from the way she moved, I thought she was about my age. That, too, stuck in my mind. Those who did come out this way were mostly old men with time on their hands, or farm workers taking a short cut across the fields to the big houses up along. Not girls in their twenties.

I followed her along the path, in that awkward proximity of strangers. I picked up my pace, feeling my black Wellingtons slip on the mud. Was I hoping to catch up with her? I'm not sure, only that she stayed precisely the same distance ahead. But when I rounded the bend in the path, she'd vanished. I stopped again, trying to work out where she'd gone. There was a trail that cut down through the reed mace to the water's edge, white stones marking a route over the mudflats at low tide. The sea was right up, though, and not even a local would reckon you could get across. I looked behind me, in case she'd doubled back, but there was no sign of her. What else? An odd smell, like rotten eggs, like seaweed on the shore in summer.

Thursday 24th November 1955, an afternoon like any other. My routine, in those days, rarely altered. On Monday and Thursday afternoons, I helped out in the library as a volunteer. It was a debt, of sorts. When I was growing up, the library was the one place I felt was mine. We had no books to speak of at home and, besides, my stepfather didn't think girls should waste time reading, but in the library I was let alone. No one shouted at me, nobody took the Mickey. Sitting cross-legged on the floor, I travelled the world in the company of Agatha Christie and Eleanor Burford and S. Rider Haggard, dreaming of being a writer myself one day. My name on the front of a book. And though nothing came of any of it – the war and our situation put paid to that – I retained an affection for the place. When I found myself back in the town twelve years later, it seemed the obvious place to work. And even now, as I stepped through the big oak doors and breathed in the familiar perfume of dust and polish, life didn't seem so bad. It was my sanctuary now, as it had been then.

That Thursday the library was closed. A burst pipe had flooded Natural Sciences and we had all been sent home. So after I'd cleared the table and the dishes were stacked and drying on the draining board, I asked our neighbour, Mrs Sadler, if she wouldn't mind staying on for a while anyway, so I could slip off.

I went out the side door, turning the handle slowly so as not to disturb him. Old habits die hard. Over the main road, quiet in the drowsy part of the afternoon, down Mill Lane and out onto the estuary, where the salt marshes lay spread out like a battered old map. When we were children, my brother forced me to climb down the bank into the muddy creek. I was scared of the black, tidal water, but I was more frightened of Harry's temper and always did what he told me. It was different on my own. Then, I could kick my heels. Bright days when the chill sun bathed the Downs in the distance in a chill yellow light. Stormy days when black clouds scud the horizon, the smell of bonfires heavy in the air. The soft days of spring, when pink ragged robin and southern marsh orchids pricked the green, or the white flowers of lady's smock, the *Collins Guide* borrowed from the Natural History section in the pocket of my regulation school coat.

We moved away when I was twelve, too young to understand the whispers or the way neighbours fell silent when my stepfather went into the Woolpack Inn. Harry signed up, went to war, and never came back. Later, I realised there had been rumours even before it happened. I had never wanted to come back, but my stepfather had been insistent and my opinion wasn't taken into account. As his mind unravelled, something had drawn him back.

There was a footbridge over the creek now. Sometimes I stopped there a while, the wooden handrail greasy beneath my fingers, and told myself that, despite it all, things were better now. Time and the war had buried the past. Wiped the slate clean.

For the next week, my stepfather's health kept me indoors. I couldn't go to work, couldn't even get out to the shops. We were locked together, he and I. One of those things. I'd always been scared of him, and he'd never shown any affection for me, now Mum was gone it fell to me to look after him. There was no one else. So it wasn't until the following Thursday, December 1st, that I went back to the marshes. I changed into my boots as I left the library, then wrapping my shoes in brown paper and putting them in my handbag, I set off along the same path. It was a blustery day and the gulls were shrieking out at sea. Only as I got out onto the marshes did I realise I'd been half looking out for her, giving her the time to show herself. But she wasn't there. As I climbed up to the flint sea wall, I was aware of a knot of disappointment in my stomach.

That afternoon, I walked all the way to Oak Pond, where an old rowing boat lay abandoned in the silted water, and the trees hung low. I smoked a cigarette and thought about some domestic worry or another, before turning back. I'd been gone longer than usual and so I hurried, knowing Mrs Sadler would be ready in her hat and coat at the door. Four o'clock, I remember looking at my wristwatch.

Then, on the far side of the silent expanse of water, I saw something flash. At first, I thought it was the lights in the library, but then I realised it was too far over. A light, right out in the middle of the marshes where Cornmill House had been. Damaged by fire and the high tides each spring, its black and rotting features had been a childhood landmark. They'd pulled it down last year, Mrs Sadler had told me. After ten years, it still attracted too many gawpers, too many ghouls. A shrine, of sorts. I narrowed my eyes. Another flash, bright, gone, then another. A signal of some kind? A shiver went down my spine and I pulled my coat tight around me, remembering how the newspaper reports claimed Cornmill House had been used as a rendez-vous long before it became notorious.

Smugglers evading the excise men, ghosts, enemy spies. I took out a local history book and read up on it. Drawings, maps of underground passages, rumours, I knew the history of the house backwards though I'd never been inside. My brother Harry boasted he'd gone in once. Seen writing on the walls and blood on the stairs, he'd said, smears on the glass where prisoners had been kept.

At first, I thought he was making it up to scare me. I didn't believe him. Later, when the police came, he denied he had ever been there. But as I listened through the crack in the door and heard him wriggle like a fish on the line, I knew for certain he had been in the house and knew the worst it had to tell. I told no one. No one asked me anyway. Harry had signed up not long after and been posted off to France. He'd died a couple of weeks later and his secret died with him.

I hadn't thought of it for years. Now, the sight of the light flashing on that cold December dusk, the memory of our old kitchen, the fug from the stove and the condensation on the inside of the windows, came rushing back. My mother's red hands twisting at her pinny and the look of calculation in my stepfather's eyes as the copper questioned Harry, and I was back there again.

I took a deep breath, in, then out. No sense in raking it all up again. The house was gone. Harry was gone, Mum too. My stepfather no longer knew who he was. And if I had seen a light where Cornmill House used to be – and already I was no longer sure – odds on it was only someone carrying a lantern over the fields to Apuldram or to the church. Nothing funny about it.

I looked for the book in the library the following Monday, but it had been taken out of circulation and there was nothing else in the local history section that caught my fancy. Besides, it was ever so busy. I had no time to think about the light on the marshes or Cornmill House. We put up the Christmas decorations. Children from the village school came to sing carols around the tree. We made paper chains.

The nights were bad that week, though. My stepfather woke two or three times between midnight and six, a bad conscience, Mrs Sadler said. So by the time the next Thursday came around, I was tired to my bones and tempted to go straight home. But, telling myself the fresh air would do me good, I set off once more along the path. A mist had come in from the sea and everything was muffled, suspended, though I could hear the suck of the tide and the call of black-headed gulls massing in the harbour. It was cold, proper December weather, and the chill seemed to soak through my woollen hat and mittens.

I'd barely gone a few steps when I noticed the smell again, the same as a fortnight ago, though far stronger. A foul stench of rotting seaweed and mud and rust. Then I heard something moving in the reeds alongside the path. Not a noise quite, more a shifting of the air. I walked faster. The sound kept pace with me, a kind of rattling, shimmering, in the rushes to my left, then a loud crack of the reed stems underfoot, as if someone was pushing their way through towards the path.

I stopped. Someone was close by, I could feel it in the pricking of my skin. Slowly, I turned round, 360 degrees, eyes pressing into the white, but not able to make anything out. Torn between turning round and going on, I took a few snatched steps more, then stopped again. Ahead of me now on the path was a figure, come out of nowhere. Blocking my way.

I gasped then with relief. It was the same woman, dressed just the same as before.

'You gave me –' I started to say, then I stopped. There was something odd in her silence and the way she was standing, her head down, hands hanging loose by her side. My heart missed a beat.

'I –'

And then I realised why she looked familiar. She was the spit of the girl who'd gone missing. They'd run her photograph on the front page of the *Observer* for weeks. And she was wearing the same WAAF uniform – green jacket, shirt and tie, pleated skirt, cap. Women's Auxiliary Airforce girls, they'd been billeted all over the village during the war.

I couldn't help it. My eyes were drawn down to her hands. I saw her gloves were torn, fragments of pale material, all in tatters at the cuffs. A matching scarf around her neck, pale pink with a red lining, coming unravelled too. No, not gloves, now I could see. Not gloves, but skin. Torn, tattered skin.

I took another step back, another, then turned and started to run. Stumbling, slipping, struggling to keep on my feet, running back along the path. I could feel her eyes on my back. I kept running, through the reed mace. Salt Mill House loomed suddenly up at me, threatening in the mist. For a moment, I thought I should stop there and ask for help. But, then, what would I say? That I'd seen a girl on the path and got the wind up. But, still, the foul smell hung about me, in my mouth, in my nose, seeping through my skin, and I couldn't stop. Didn't dare to stop.

I was out on the mudflats now, treacherous in the dusk. My boots sank lower at each step. The mud was like clawing hands around my ankles, trying to drag me down. Out here, pockets of swamp lay concealed amongst the reeds, sinking mud and false land where a person could be pulled down into the estuary. Flecks of grass, of seaweed, of sludge splattered up onto the back of my legs and skirt and hem of my coat. My throat was sore from running, burning like a slug of whisky in a child's mouth, but panic kept me going, deeper into the marsh. On across the eel grass, where the savannah sparrows nested, over the samphire, faded at the tail of the year, past the creek, until finally Mill Lane was in sight and the solid, familiar outline of the library.

Finally, I stopped running, put my hand against the familiar bricks, to catch my breath. I looked behind me. Nothing was there, no one. I realised the smell had gone. The mist was also beginning to lift. I don't know how long I stood there, only that already I was embarrassed at how I'd let my imagination get the better of me. That girl, whoever she was, what must she think? I took one look, then turned tail. She'd think I was mad. So what if she was dressed in rather old-fashioned clothes? And as for the marks on her wrists, just a trick of the light in the fading afternoon. She'd hardly have been walking around otherwise, would she?

I hesitated for a moment. I was late already and I looked a sketch. Salt water splashed up the back of my raincoat, my gloves stiff with mud. Mrs Sadler would be sure to pass comment, she was the type who didn't let anything go. But there was something I had to do, read, before I went home. I wouldn't rest else. Mrs Sadler would have to wait.

Quickly, I walked up the steps and into the library. To my relief, Albert was still on the front desk, his glasses perched on the tip of his red nose.

'Back again?' he said.

'You know me, Bert, can't keep away.'

'Something I can help you with, love?'

'No it's all right. I can manage. I'll be five minutes.'

'Take as long as you like,' the old man said, dabbing at his nose with his handkerchief. 'No hurry.'

I rushed through the stacks to the archive room at the back of the building, where back issues of local and parish newspapers were kept. Floor to ceiling hanging files and oversize drawers, nothing had been put onto film yet. In the middle, a large central desk with drawers, the desk large enough to accommodate ten people working at any one time. I cast my eyes over the years, months, weeks, until I found the box I needed. Then, with my heart going nineteen to the dozen, I flicked through until I found the edition I wanted.

The black and white eyes of the murdered girl looked out at me. The brown hair beneath the cap, the belted jacket and pleated skirt, shirt and tie. I caught my breath. And beneath the description of the murder, her throat cut from ear to ear. The marks on wrists suggesting she'd been kept captive for a while before she died.

I slumped down on the chair, the photograph bringing the events of that night back. The whispers, the pointed fingers, the speculation. After the police had gone, Mum and my stepfather arguing in whispers, so the neighbours wouldn't hear through the walls. She took Harry's side. Said they were talking to every man over sixteen, nothing sinister about it. Bound to be one of the soldiers billeted at Oakwood or Goodwood. Besides, what respectable girl would go on her own, to a place like that? Asking for trouble.

Slowly, I put the newspapers away, turned off the light and left.

'All done?' said Bert.

I nodded. 'I'll be getting off home. See you Monday.'

'Have a nice weekend, love.'

'You too.'

I walked back up Mill Lane, then crossed over to the road where we lived. The back door was unlocked. I took off my boots and hung my coat, inside out, on the back of the door, before calling out.

'It's only me,' I said, going through to the hall. 'Sorry I'm late.'

Mrs Sadler was dressed for outside, hat and gloves on, hands folded in front of her. She glanced pointedly at the clock on the windowsill by the sink.

'How's he been?'

'He's been all worked up this afternoon. Talking about some girl and your brother Harry, too. Mind you, it's hard to know what he's saying half the time. And his language, I don't mind telling you –'

'Has he had his tea?' I said, more sharply than I intended.

'At four, as usual. When you weren't back, I thought I'd better.'

Her voice was begrudging, hard done by.

'Yes, thanks. And for staying late. I'll see you Monday?'

A sly look crossed her broad face. 'I don't know. Mr Sadler doesn't like me coming here, you know how he is.'

I was tempted to say, no I didn't know, but I was still more shaken up than I cared to admit and, besides, who else would come in and sit with my stepfather? I went to my purse, got out a five-bob note, and put it on the table. Would that help matters indoors, I asked? I could see her thinking about it, totting up the extra shillings. She held out a moment longer, then her hand reached out and took it.

'See you Monday then,' she said.

After she'd gone, I locked the back door and since there was no one about to see, stepped out of my skirt and sponged the mud as best I could. While it dried, I put on my old gardening skirt that was hanging over the back of the chair where I'd been mending it earlier. I looked at the clock. Only five o'clock and already it was black as pitch. I leaned over the sink and pulled on the curtains to shut out the dark. The wire was old and the fabric too heavy, so they stuck half way, as they usually did, leaving a slat of silver light coming in from the light in the alley that ran along the back of the cottages.

At seven o'clock, I took a tin of soup from the larder and put a saucepan on the stove, cut two slices of bread and buttered them, then put a piece of cheddar on the side of our plates. We ate our meal in silence and the evening dragged, as it always did. I put on the wireless to keep him company. I picked up a novel I'd been reading, but it didn't hold my attention. I couldn't stop thinking about the newspaper article, about my brother, about all the worry that had sent my mum into an early grave.

My stepfather was restless, talking, mumbling, drifting in and out of sleep. Looking at him now, I wondered at how I'd ever been so scared of him. He'd been a big man in his day, working at the Anglesey Arms in Halnaker after we'd moved from here, until that job, like all the others, fell through. He called them misunderstandings, said everyone was out to get him, but the plain truth was he was a drunk. After that, he never worked again. He just sat about the house with a bottle in one hand, cigarette in the other, picking fights with any of us stupid enough to get in his way.

At nine o'clock, I put him to bed – he slept downstairs now – then went back into the front room to get things straight for the morning, as if it mattered. Nobody but Mrs Sadler and the vicar ever visited. I turned off the table lamp, then went back through to the kitchen to get a glass of water to take up with me. Except for the corridor of light coming in through the gap in the curtains, the room was dark. The cold tap spluttered, the pipes complaining, so I let it run a moment. Then, through the gap in the curtains, I swear I saw something move in the yard. My heart lurched. I put down the glass on the draining board and leaned forward to look out. Nothing, just my own reflection looking back at me in the cold glass. I knew I'd locked the back door earlier, but I glanced over all the same to be sure. The key, which I always left in the door, was gone.

Telling myself not to be so jittery, I crouched down. I ran my fingers over the coarse mat and was relieved when my fingers connected with the cold metal. Odd it should have fallen out. I shot the bolts top and bottom, just to be sure, then picked up my glass and went back into the cold hallway.

I caught my breath. Then sighed. 'You gave me a fright, Dad,' I said.

My stepfather was standing in the corridor, swaying slightly on his feet.

'What are you doing up?' I said, not expecting an answer. 'You'll catch your death.'

'She's here.'

'What did you say?' I gasped, astonished he'd spoken. Then I saw his eyes. Clear for the first time in years, unclouded, and fixed at a point behind me.

'She's come,' he said again.

'Who's come, Dad?'

But even as I said it, of course I knew. I could feel the prickling on my skin at the back of my neck, my hands. And the smell of the shore at low tide. I didn't want to look round, but I couldn't stop myself.

Slowly I turned round, to face the girl I knew was standing behind me. The skin at her wrists, rubbed raw where the wire had cut through. The ragged red seam where his knife had dragged across her throat, right to left. The work of a left-handed man. Not Harry. For all his faults, not Harry.

For an instant, I saw her clearly, both the girl she had been and the girl she now was, twelve years dead, lying in the churchyard with a headstone at her feet. Then slowly, she began to lift her head, the same steady and deliberate movement as on the path earlier.

This time, I forced myself not to look away. Then a rush of air, cold and damp like the mist on the marshes, as if someone had opened a door and let the night in. And a dreadful howling, like a deer caught in a mantrap. Only afterwards did I learn that sound came from my lips. The girl smiled, then her features, printed pretty on the front page of the newspaper all those years ago, began to change, collapsing in upon themselves. Brown eyes becoming white, red lips shrivelling to black, her skin a spider's web of veins and blood.

Suddenly, she leapt. I screamed, hitting at the air with useless hands, to protect myself or protect him, I couldn't say. But he didn't resist. His legs buckled and he fell forward, arms by his side, making no attempt to break the fall. Then silence, stillness.

I sank to the ground, knees drawn up to my chin, oblivious to the blood seeping across the tiles and soaking into the hem of my skirt. I don't know how long I lay there, we lay there, only that I gradually became aware of banging on the front door and someone calling my name. Later, they told me it was my screaming that alerted the neighbours something was wrong. That, and a strange smell of rotting seaweed permeating through the thin cottage walls.

The doctor said it was a heart attack. A blessing,

he called it, that he went so fast. Here one minute, gone the next. Just like that. I said nothing. I knew now he had been dying for years. Waiting, all that time, for her to come and claim him.

And what of me? I stayed, of course. I wrote about it, not what happened that night, but about the murder. Sitting in the lending library, surrounded by all the newspaper articles and history books. In my own small way, I became quite well known. My book sits alongside all those writers I used to admire, which was all I ever wanted really. And, on winter nights, the lights still shine out across the fields, a sanctuary for anyone who needs a safe place to go.

(A version of this story was first published as 'The Revenant' in two instalments in *The Big Issue*, December 2009.)

FIGHT FOR LIBRARIES AS YOU DO FREEDOM

KARIN SLAUGHTER

My father and his eight siblings grew up in the kind of poverty that America doesn't like to talk about unless something like Katrina happens, and then the conversation only lasts as long as the news cycle. His family squatted in shacks. The children scavenged the forest for food. They put cardboard over empty windowpanes so the cold wouldn't kill them.

Books did not exist here. When your kids are starving, you can't point with pride to a book you've just spent six hours reading. Picking cotton, sewing flour bags into clothes – those were the skills my father grew up appreciating.

And yet, when he noticed that I, his youngest daughter, showed an interest in reading, he took me to our local Jonesboro library and told me that I could read any book in the building so long as I promised to talk to him about it if I read something I didn't understand. I think this is the greatest gift my father ever gave me. Though he was not a reader himself, he understood that reading is not just an escape. It is access to a better way of life.

But, why do we need to read? It's not a survival skill. Contrary to how some of us feel, we won't die if we can't read. I think the need for reading boils down to one simple issue: children are selfish. Reading about other people creates a sense of balance in a child's life. It gives them the knowledge that there is a world outside themselves. It tells them that the language they are learning at home is the key to unlocking the mysteries of the greater world.

Reading develops cognitive skills. It trains your mind to question what you are told, which is why the first thing dictators do when they come to power is censor or ban books. It's why it was illegal for so many years to teach slaves to read. It's why girls in developing countries have acid thrown in their faces going to school.

You would just as soon cut *Romeo and Juliet* from a high school curriculum as you would cut algebra. Both train young minds how to think in critical ways. Both foster problem solving and spatial reasoning. Both create adults who question and contribute to society. Fundamentally, reading creates better societies. This is not a theory. This is a quantifiable fact: there is a direct correlation between the rate of literacy in a nation and its success.

This is why the funding of libraries should be a matter of national security. Keeping libraries open, giving access to all children to all books is vital to our nation's sovereignty. For nearly 85 percent of kids living in rural areas, the only place where they have access to technology or books outside the schoolroom is in a public library. For many urban kids, the only safe haven they have to study or do homework is the public library. Librarians are soldiers in the battle for our place in the world, and in many cases they are getting the least amount of support our communities can offer.

We need to shift our national view of libraries not as luxuries, but as necessities. When tragedy strikes in other nations, we are generous, but our libraries are being hit with a tsunami and there has been no call to action. Staff are being fired. Hours are being cut. Doors are being closed. Buildings are being razed. Kids are being left behind. Futures are being destroyed.

Libraries are the backbone of our educational infrastructure, and they are being slowly broken by bankrupt local governments and apathetic politicians. As voters and taxpayers, we have to demand that our local governments properly prioritise libraries. As charitable citizens, we must invest in our library down the street so that the generations serviced by that library grow up to be adults who contribute not just to their local communities, but to the world.

Kids who read become students who do well in

school. Students who do well in school go to college. College students graduate to good jobs and pay higher taxes. Libraries don't service only left-wingers or right. They don't judge by class, race or religion. They service everyone in their community, no matter their circumstances. Rich or poor; no one is denied. Libraries are not simply part of our guarantee to the pursuit of happiness. They are a civil right. If we lose our libraries, we risk losing our communities, our families and ourselves.

(Reprinted with permission of The *Atlanta Journal-Constitution*.)

AFTERWORD

MIRANDA MCKEARNEY

In Tower Hamlets, I join a library's weekly story time, alongside a flood of families with under fives – speaking the most fantastic mix of languages.

Then on to St Helens, where I talk to a crowd of young people, who've been working on a community Reading and Writing Roadshow. It's based in the central library, aimed at other teens, and they all share it through Facebook and Twitter.

At Catford Library, Louis Howell describes the months he's spent helping younger children get through the Summer Reading Challenge. They've now read six whole books – and the staff say Louis has built up a bit of a cult following. The readers are mostly young Afro-Caribbean boys, previously reluctant to read.

Swansea Library has a sensational view out to

sea, as well as a cheeringly young and enthusiastic staff – who love to share stories about their reading support work. Their book displays are vibrant, their reading groups well attended, they host excitingly diverse author events and help introduce people to the worldwide web as well as words on paper.

And then in Sevenoaks, librarians tell me about running an experimental event, where the author attended via Skype. We talk about it while the knitting club meets alongside us.

Everywhere you go in the UK, there's a library, right at the heart of the community. Helping people research their family history; find a poem for a funeral; get online for the first time; use the space for community meetings; meet an author or introduce their baby to the rhythms of language.

The Reading Agency is an independent charity with a mission to inspire more people to read more. We aim to drive up participation in reading so that everyone has the intellectual freedom, life chances and sheer joy and inspiration that comes when life is full of books. We're all lucky enough to be confident readers, but many people struggle with low literacy skills. We're passionate about helping everyone have the chance to become a confident reader, and we specialise in working with libraries to spread reading, because libraries offer every single member of the community free and equal access.

It's inspirational for us. Libraries have a radical, socially equalising role right across the UK, and we support that by developing practical tools and training to take their work further. The proceeds of this book will go to sustaining and developing our two reading challenge schemes – the Six Book Challenge for adults, and the Summer Reading Challenge for children. Libraries use these schemes to encourage people to enjoy reading, often for the first time.

Mary did the Six Book Challenge through the library in Shoreham after enquiring about adult education courses through her children's school. Having experienced severe post-natal depression she was trying to get back on track – and back into work, too.

'I had really lost confidence in myself and I hadn't picked up a book since I was about twenty-five. I just didn't think, what with being a mum to three children, that I'd be able to carve out the time to get started again. The idea of reading a whole book from start to finish seemed impossible, and I was worried that I would make a fool of myself.

'Despite all my fears, I did give the Six Book Challenge a go and found myself hooked.

'I'd thought I didn't have the intelligence or the confidence or the concentration to be able to understand what a writer was trying to get across in a book, or be able to discuss that in a group, but I found I could. It was fantastic, after all those years of not having picked up a book.

'I carried on with the Six Book Challenge . . . and

went on to read twelve books! Now I am reading every day, when the kids are in bed, or when they are having a nap or even in the car. Completing the Six Book Challenge gave me the confidence to go on and get the qualifications I need: I am training to be a teaching assistant. And now we read every day as a family. My sense of achievement from doing the Six Book Challenge has done wonders for my confidence. It gave me the focus I needed to go on and do everything else.'

Every day, across the country, there are transformations like this. Libraries are the place where reading comes alive in the community. It's both heartwarming and heartbreaking to see local communities fight to keep their library open, and a reminder of just what they mean to people. Authors, of all kinds of books, have been standing alongside readers of all ages, classes and backgrounds, championing libraries, and the contributions included here are full of that passion. What leaps out is how essential libraries are to the written word – and how they open up the world for everyone, writers and readers alike.

We believe it's vital that in campaigning to save our irreplaceable public library network we look to the future as well as the past. Libraries must evolve to survive. The work of The Reading Agency is focused on helping libraries become the place where local people can go for rich, inspiring experiences that will help them become readers for life.

In these difficult times, I hold in my mind my recent visit to Rotherham's new Riverside Library a few months before its opening – the vibrant colours of the carpets being laid, light flooding in, a state-of-the-art computer suite and playful children's area. We need these reading places in our communities, from Rotherham to Ramsgate, Redcar to Reigate. Let it not be on our watch that we lose them.

(Miranda McKearney OBE is the Chief Executive of The Reading Agency.)

To support The Reading Agency, visit
www.readingagency.org.uk

CONTRIBUTORS

Anita Anand presents Double Take on BBC Radio 5 Live. Previously she presented the BBC's Daily Politics, and 5 Live Drive. She has anchored The World Today and Outlook on BBC World Service, and Saturday Live and Midweek for BBC Radio 4. Anita has also been a columnist for *India Today* and *The Asian Age* as well as the *Guardian*. She lives in London.

Julian Barnes has written ten novels and three collections of short stories. In 2011 he won the Man Booker Prize for *The Sense of an Ending*. He lives in London.

Bella Bathurst is a writer, journalist and photographer. Her first book, *The Lighthouse Stevensons*, won the Somerset Maugham Prize. Her most recent book is *The Bicycle Book*.

Alan Bennett is the author of *Untold Stories*, and numerous works of fiction including *The Uncommon Reader*. His play *The History Boys* was the National Theatre's most successful production ever.

Michael Brooks is the author of the bestselling non-fiction title *13 Things That Don't Make Sense*. He holds a PhD in quantum physics, is a consultant at *New Scientist* and writes a weekly column for the *New Statesman*.

James Brown started his career at the *NME* and then created *Loaded* magazine. He was once voted more influential than Mrs Thatcher and the Pope by Channel 4 and the *Observer* (who were clearly on drugs at the time). He now publishes www.sabotagetimes.com

Ann Cleeves worked as a probation officer, bird observatory cook and auxiliary coastguard before she started writing full-time. In 2006 she was awarded the Duncan Lawrie Dagger for Best Crime Novel, for *Raven Black*. ITV's adaptation of her Vera Stanhope novels stars Brenda Blethyn. She lives in North Tyneside.

Stephen Fry is an award-winning actor, writer and presenter. He rose to fame alongside Hugh Laurie in *A Bit of Fry and Laurie* and *Jeeves and Wooster*, and was unforgettable as General Melchett in *Blackadder*. More recently he presented *Stephen*

Fry: The Secret Life of the Manic Depressive. His legions of fans tune in to watch him host the popular quiz show *QI* each week. His biography *The Fry Chronicles*, spanning the years 1979–1987, was the bestselling non-fiction hardback of 2010.

Seth Godin is the author of *Tribes*, *The Dip*, *Purple Cow*, *Linchpin* and other international bestsellers. He is the most influential business blogger in the world, and the founder and CEO of Squidoo.com. He lives in Westchester, New York.

Susan Hill is the author of the literary memoir *Howards End is on the Landing* and the ghost stories *The Woman in Black*, *The Man in the Picture* and *The Small Hand*. She also writes the successful Simon Serailler crime series.

Tom Holland is the author of three works of history: *Rubicon*, *Persian Fire* and *Millennium*. His new book, *In the Shadow of the Sword* – about late antiquity and the origins of Islam – is out in 2012.

Hardeep Singh Kohli is a comedian, journalist, broadcaster and author of *Indian Takeaway*. He appears regularly across BBC Radio 2 and 4.

Lucy Mangan is a feature writer for the *Guardian* and the author of *Hopscotch and Handbags*, *The Reluctant Bride* and *My Family and Other Disasters*.

Val McDermid grew up in a Scottish mining community; she then read English at Oxford. She was a journalist for sixteen years, spending the last three as Northern Bureau Chief of a national Sunday tabloid. She divides her time between Northumberland and Cheshire and has published twenty-five novels.

China Miéville lives and works in London. He is three-time winner of the Arthur C. Clarke Award and has also won the Hugo and World Fantasy Award. His most recent novel, *Embassytown*, was published in 2011.

Caitlin Moran is an award-winning writer and broadcaster. She has worked extensively on television as well as national press, in addition to writing *How to Be a Woman*. She currently writes a weekly column for *The Times*.

Kate Mosse is the author of three non-fiction books, two plays and five novels, including the bestseller, *Labyrinth*. The third novel in her Languedoc Trilogy, *Citadel*, will be published in 2012. The Co-Founder & Honorary Director of the Orange Prize for Fiction, she is also Co-Director of the Chichester Writing Festival and a board member of the National Theatre.

Julie Myerson is the author of eight novels, including

Something Might Happen, and three works of non-fiction, including *Home: The Story of Everyone Who Ever Lived In Our House*, and *The Lost Child*. She lives in London and Suffolk with her husband and teenage children.

Bali Rai was born in Leicester in 1971 and grew up in a multicultural, multi-racial community close to the city centre. He writes novels about young adults as well as the successful Soccer Squad series.

Lionel Shriver's novels include *We Need to Talk About Kevin*, *So Much for That* and *A Perfectly Good Family*. Her writing has appeared in the *Guardian*, *New York Times* and many other publications. She lives in London.

Karin Slaughter is an internationally bestselling author of several novels, including the Grant County series and the Will Trent series. She is the founder of the Save the Libraries project, which has raised nearly $100k for libraries worldwide.

Zadie Smith was born in north-west London in 1975. She is the author of the novels *White Teeth*, *The Autograph Man* and *On Beauty*, and the essay collection *Changing My Mind*, all of which are published by Penguin.

Robin Turner is one of the editors of the Caught by

the River website and the recently published book, *A Collection of Words on Water*. He co-authored *The Rough Pub Guide* and is currently working on the follow-up.

Nicky Wire is the bass player and lyricist with the Manic Street Preachers. The group have released ten critically acclaimed albums over two decades, during which time they have won – amongst others – four Brits, an Ivor Novello, five Q awards, the *Mojo* Maverick award and the *NME*'s coveted Godlike Genius Award.

ACKNOWLEDGEMENTS

With thanks to Miranda McKearney, Peter Barker, Sandeep Mahal, Harpreet Purewal, Isobel Frankish and all at The Reading Agency; Benedicte Page at *The Bookseller*; Marigold Atkey, Bernadette Baker-Baughman, Sarah Ballard, John Bulloch, Pat Burgess, Mic Cheetham, Lottie Fyfe, Georgia Garrett, Jane Gregory, Victoria Hobbs, Victoria Sanders, Craig Tregurtha, Claire Weatherhead, Helen Wilson; all at Profile Books, and all the authors who gave their work.

With thanks to the following for the use of material:

Guardian for Bella Bathurst, Lionel Shriver, Nicky Wire

ACKNOWLEDGEMENTS

London Review of Books for Alan Bennett

Macmillan Publishers for China Miéville

The Times for Caitlin Moran

The Writers' and Artists' Yearbook, A&C Black for Julie Myerson